D0451573

Weight Management for Triathletes

by Ingrid Loos Miller

Meyer & Meyer Sport

IRON**MAN**® is a registered trademark of World Triathlon Corporation

British Library Cataloguing in Publication Data
A catalogue record for this book is available from the British Library

Ingrid Loos Miller, Weight Management for Triathletes
Maidenhead: Meyer & Meyer Sport (UK) Ltd., 2010
ISBN 978-1-84126-290-1

© 2010 by Meyer & Meyer Sport (UK) Ltd.
Aachen, Adelaide, Auckland, Budapest, Cape Town, Graz, Indianpolis,
Maidenhead, New York, Olten (CH), Singapore, Toronto
 Member of the World
Sport Publishers' Association (WSPA)
www.w-s-p-a.org
Printed and bound by: B.O.S.S Druck und Medien GmbH, Germany
ISBN 978-1-84126-290-1
E-Mail: info@m-m-sports.com
www.m-m-sports.com

Contents

PREFACE

I was first introduced to the world of peer-reviewed scientific papers in college. One of the first ones I read was about mice and appetite. The researchers put hundreds of little mice on a wheel and watched them go round and round. Most of the mice lost weight because of the extra exercise, but some of them didn't. They weren't lazy; they ran just as much as the other mice. The mice that didn't lose weight ate *just enough* extra food to compensate for the exercise. They were master compensators.

This book is for master compensators, the "MC athletes." Only in our overly abundant world is this tendency a hindrance. Mice don't care how fat they are, but people do. Those among us who have our fat thermostats set too high suffer with it our whole lives, but we are not mice. We can, with great effort, overcome our natural tendencies.

In the world of triathlon, the MCs train heavily but stay heavy. One of them told me, "it is nearly impossible for me to control what I eat, but I'm not afraid to sweat a lot."

The information superhighway of triathlon is dominated by former champions who have turned their celebrity into coaching careers, and by dieticians that talk about sports nutrition and using fuel to maximize performance – not Master Compensators.

What is entirely missing from the triathlete's information stream is help with the day-to-day challenge of eating less than your body wants. The challenges faced by an MC athlete go well beyond calorie counting. They face temptation in every environment, even during training sessions where advertisers push a buffet of carbohydrate replacements. An MC athlete must carve his way through his habits, his psychology and various social expectations. The triathlon world does not provide MCs with the tools to manage it all. This book does.

The emphasis on improving performance creates a conflict for triathletes that want to lose weight. Everything is done with performance in mind and heaven forbid if something else takes center stage. It is not possible or advisable to lose weight and at the same time, force the physiological adaptations that will make you a faster, stronger athletic machine. Weight loss is an adaptation – *an adaptation to starvation*. That is plenty for your body to deal with. What's more, the adaptations come more easily with a program that takes weight off relatively quickly. Losing a bit of muscle is part of the process. If you want to lose fat, you will lose some muscle too. But that is not the end of the world. You will get it back. A focused weight loss plan will produce results and you need to see results to stick with the plan.

Triathletes take pride in being different from non-athletes. But triathletes that are Master Compensators will lose weight only when they can cross back into the real world and use the tools that work for non-athletes. This gives them the boost that, along with their training, pushes them past the MC blockade. It requires a mental shift that triathletes resist, but once they make the move, their drive to train gets them to their destination faster than most. The training also helps MCs keep the weight off.

Losing weight to become faster takes the same skills, focus and dedication as losing weight to fit into your jeans. I wrote this book to show triathletes how to incorporate traditional weight loss tools into their unique world. The information is based on my personal experience as an MC athlete. It is based on a lifetime of study, experimentation, failure and shared experience with hundreds of Master Compensators, mostly through the WeightWatchers® program. Exceptionally qualified contributors have added their expertise and where possible, scientific references have been provided. The result is a guide that is based on experience and science.

I am not a psychologist, dietician or an elite athlete. I have lost 45 pounds and kept it off. That accomplishment has been harder won than any Ironman could ever be. An elemental shift in understanding the problem was the first critical step. The second was gathering the weapons needed for battle – and don't be fooled into thinking that weight loss is anything less for Master Compensators. I hope this book will lead you successfully through both steps.

I maintain active websites and welcome your questions, comments and success stories.

www.weightmanagementfortriathletes.com
www.ironplanner.net
www.ingridloosmiller.com

Happy Training, Ingrid

PART 1 – LOOKING AHEAD
INTRODUCTION: WHAT IS IN THIS BOOK

Losing weight is about managing food. This book will teach you how to lose weight in the context of the sport of triathlon.

There are plenty of nutrition books around. So if you want to know about vitamins and nutrients, look elsewhere. This book picks up where nutrition books leave off, providing the detailed strategies and information you need to successfully implement a weight loss program.

Trying to lose weight and train hard at the same time is futile. Either your training suffers, or you don't lose weight. You can't do both things well at the same time. This guide encourages athletes to temporarily make weight loss the first priority. Training at modest levels breaks the "train to eat" cycle and allows brisk weight loss. After you have reached your body composition goals, you can return to making training the priority.

The book is for triathletes of all levels who want to lose body fat. A variety of approaches will suit athletes looking to lose a few pounds as well as those wanting to make more significant changes. Below is a summary of the chapters so you can get started with what interests you most.

PART 1: LOOKING AHEAD

Chapter 1: Expectations – prepares you for the rigors of weight loss, describing common expectations and how they compare with reality, what to expect about weight loss being easy, rate of weight loss, maintaining muscle, how you will look, maintaining your goal weight, and differences between the sexes when it comes to weight loss.

PART 2: BODY COMPOSITION

Chapter 2: How Important Is it to Be Lean? – explains how important low body fat is for triathlon performance. Exercise physiologist and coach Alan Couzens provides detailed analysis including time improvement predictions for various race distances.

Chapter 3: Where Do You Stand? – is about the body mass index and body composition testing. Various methods are described along with their particular limitations and how to use body fat data and the scale to monitor progress.

Chapter 4: Three Goals – learn about the 3 goals that will get you to your new normal weight; lose, maintain and stabilize. How to decide what the numbers should be, how body composition shifts over time and determining your ideal body composition for performance and aesthetics.

PART 3: MANAGING FOOD

Chapter 5: Your Calorie Target – why you need a calorie target and how to use it. Shortcut calorie targets are provided if you don't want to bother with calculations.

Chapter 6: Keeping Track – defines several eating styles and explains 3 simple ways to track what you eat: calorie counting, the visual plate and clean foods. Examples, pros and cons of each method are included.

Chapter 7: Three Skills – is about how to limit, substitute and modify high calorie density food so you can continue to eat what you enjoy and still lose weight. Create a food list of what you currently eat. Use the list to identify problem foods and as a calorie reference.

Chapter 8: Tools for Success – explains daily practices and numerous tools to manage hunger, social situations and dining-out.

PART 4: TRAINING FUEL

Chapter 9: Train to Lose – training intensity, strength training and trouble-shooting fueling guidelines so you can train moderately and lose weight without starving.

Chapter 10: The Ironman Trap – discusses the unique needs of triathletes training for Ironman distance races. How to avoid the overeating habit while fueling adequately for performance and recovery.

PART 5: MINDSET

Chapter 11: Success Stories – has the stories of professional triathlete Matt Lieto and an age-grouper, "Scott," who overcame addiction and obesity.

Chapter 12: Motivation – using motivation to stick with your weight loss plan. Topics include moving away from pain, triggers, the pull of success, what you really want, what drives you, the success cycle, arrival, mental mastery and celebrating victory.

Chapter 13: Action – the decision to lose weight is the catalyst for change. The importance of urgency, persistence, tenacity, prioritizing and celebrating success are discussed.

PART 6: RELATED SUBJECTS

Chapter 14: Weight Divisions – the history and politics of weight divisions, who they are for, how they came about and their influence on the sport. The Clyde handicap is described and there is an interview with Professional Triathlete Heather Wurtele.

Chapter 15: Weight-Loss Supplements – is about using caution with weight loss supplements. Describes regulations, contamination, and a table summarizing claims and efficacy of common supplements.

Chapter 16: What Can Surgery Do? – discusses weight-loss related surgery. Statistics, moral dilemmas, athletes as patients, where to start, adjusting to a new you and accepting the body you have.

Chapter 17: Going too Far – is about the difference between dedicated athleticism and psychological disorders including exercise addiction, anorexia, bulimia and binge-eating, the female athlete triad and body dysmorphic disorder.

1 Expectations

We advance on our journey only when we face our goal,
when we are confident and believe we are going to win out.

– Orison Swett Marden

REALITY CHECK

It is helpful and important to know what you are in for when you decide to lose weight. If you are like most people, you have tried before and have probably succeeded to a degree. But as time goes on you have found yourself at the beginning of a weight loss program again and again, each time more disheartened that you have still not succeeded.

Don't despair. This is the last time you will be here. This time you will be prepared. This time your goal will be for lifetime weight management, not just a number on the scale. This time you will go into it with accurate expectations and an unstoppable attitude. This time you will be patient and informed and this time you will have the magnetism of triathlon to pull you through the rough spots. This time you have a dream. Like buying a fast wetsuit and having a professional bike fit, the quest for leanness it is an inevitable step in the evolution of a triathlete. Welcome to the next step.

It starts with realizing that in triathlon and in life, you learn more from your mistakes than from your victories. Your entire weight management history has prepared you for *this* final push. Let's start with some common misconceptions about weight loss.

EXPECTING TRAINING TO BE ENOUGH

When a newbie starts training, he loses some weight, gets fit and feels great. "With all this training," he figures, "I'll be rid of this spare tire by summer." His race resume grows along with the number of triathlon-related doo-dads he owns. Investing in the sport brings improvement, but summer comes and goes and the spare tire remains.

Sometimes changes don't come fast enough. Body dissatisfaction is common among triathletes, especially beginners who wonder. "How long does it take to look like a machine? I'm 21% body fat but in my opinion, that's not good enough. I look at 'normal' non-athletic women, and even though I'm leaner than most; it is irrelevant when it comes to racing and there's lean, ripped awesome athletes strutting their stuff in lycra. Basically, I'm a fat triathlete."

If training was enough, you would not be reading this book. It would be nice if training was all you needed to keep the weight off, but it isn't. The human body fights mightily against starvation and weight loss [1]. Training isn't going to change that if you are a person that tends to hold on to weight. It is entirely possible, even common, to (inadvertently) increase your calorie intake *just enough* to offset the calorie deficit created by an 8, 10, or 14-hour training week. Women are especially good at this; they are probably wired that way.

If you want to lose weight, you need to change your attitude. The change in attitude will get you moving in the right direction. Forget you are an athlete. Yes, it is so important that I'll say it again.

Forget you are an athlete.

I don't mean it literally. I mean stop focusing on training, training and more training to solve your problem. Focus on *food*. Focus on how to eat fewer calories than your body wants. If you don't do this, the weight will not come off. "Forgetting you are an athlete" is a mental shift that will force you to manage your weight just like your couch-potato neighbor, your boss, or the gals at WeightWatchers®. You need to go over to that "other side" for a little while. The pay off will be tremendous.

Up until now you have been focused on training and eating "reasonably," whatever that means. Once you start to keep track of your food, you will see that "reasonable" eating is overeating. You will also, sadly, realize why obesity is everywhere and getting worse. People on average eat *way too many calories.*

We are triathletes because we love the sport, the training and the challenge. But we don't want to become slaves to it. What if some calamity forced you to take some time away from training, how fast would you put on weight? The goal of this book is to help you control your eating so well that you could take a few weeks away from training without putting on more than a pound or two.

By learning to eat *as if* you were not training at all, you will solve two problems: you will stop being a slave to your training and you will lose weight quickly. Both of these steps are necessary. You have to take control of food so it no longer calls the shots.

You should continue to train for 6-8 hours per week. Non-athletes that successfully maintain a significant weight loss typically exercise this long too, so it is a good baseline to establish. Be careful, if you add more training hours you may start needing "recovery meals" and "carbohydrate replacements" which will slow your progress (see Chapter 9). Don't worry, you can go back to all of that later. For now, losing weight is the goal.

EXPECTING WEIGHT LOSS TO BE EASY, QUICK OR BOTH

A moderate approach to weight loss will only get you so far. If you are reading this book, odds are you have already tried moderation and it has not been enough. If you have been fighting weight most of your life, your biology is against you and you need to get serious to overcome it.

> Extremism in pursuit of permanent lifestyle change is no vice.
> Moderation in defense of failure to change is no virtue.
>
> – *Daniel S. Kirschenbaum, PhD in The 9 Truths about Weight Loss*

Taking a more extreme approach to weight loss will give you better results. How extreme? Extreme enough that you are completely (not moderately) dedicated to success. Losing 1-2 pounds a week, week after week until you are leaner than you have ever been as an adult is pretty extreme. But it is worth it.

Eating less than you use is a simple concept. Figuring out how to do it day after day without starving yourself, as your motivation waxes and wanes, is really hard. If you tend to be overweight, you are fighting biology and that biology stays with you even after you have reached your goal. You will have to deal with your weight forever.

Kirschenbaum, quoted above, writes, "…weight controllers shape their bodies into super normal condition via exceptional personal management skills, they deserve praise and support for their efforts. … Essentially, weight control is a major athletic challenge." [2] When you think of weight management as an athletic challenge, you realize it will require daily, lifetime attention. You already have the skills of an athlete so it is a matter of applying that drive and persistence to losing weight.

EXPECTING TO LOSE WEIGHT EVERY WEEK

As training for an Ironman is a journey, weight loss is as well. There are weeks when you will lose a surprising amount of weight, and weeks when the scale (undeservedly) goes up. Plateaus, dips and climbs are the order of the day. It is typical to lose faster in the first week or two before things level off. The initial weight loss is mostly water but the amount of fat you lose each week will stay constant if you continue to stay within your calorie target. On *average* you should lose 1-2 pounds a week, but the road is never smooth and straight. Stepping on the scale often and recording the result demonstrates how variable weight can be from day to day, even with steady adherence to a weight loss plan. Daily weight can vary 5 pounds without necessarily reflecting a change in the rate of fat loss.

Calculating calorie deficits does not predict short term weight loss very well. Theoretically, you could reduce daily intake by 100 calories per day and in one year, lose about ten pounds! But it doesn't work that way and that is why modest attempts at weight loss fail. Yes, calories do count, but you won't see changes on the scale until you create a big calorie deficit in a *few days*. The deficit needs to come from limiting food, not from exercise. Your body needs a big shove (calorie deficit) to get things moving.

You will know the weight loss is starting when you have a day of urinating more than usual. That is the signal that water is being lost. The water loss signals that the process has begun and the scale will confirm it. The initial loss is primarily water but as time goes on, proportionally more fat is burned. The numbers on the scale will vary but the *rate of fat loss will continue steadily* as long as you create a calorie deficit. [3]

EXPECTING TO MAINTAIN ALL OF YOUR MUSCLE

Losing some muscle is unavoidable during weight loss. This is in part because as you become lighter, the body no longer needs as much muscle to move it around. Be prepared for this adjustment. If you take an overly conservative approach to weight loss to avoid losing muscle, it will take too long and your motivation will falter. Motivation is the most important tool you have. Lose the weight first. You can regain the muscle after you have reached your goal and when you return to training for performance.

When *calorie restriction alone* is used for weight loss, up to 25% of weight loss is muscle. This relatively high rate of muscle loss levels off after a few weeks [4]. Your program will not be based on calorie restriction alone, you will be training too. Here are some things you can do to minimize muscle loss.

1. Continue to train. This will reduce the muscle loss. [5, 6] The training should not be excessively long, about 6 hours per week. Strength training is as important as your other training when it comes to weight loss. [7] While aerobic work is primarily calorie burning, strength training burns calories and builds (or helps maintain) calorie burning muscle. Think of it as an investment. The work you do in the gym will help you now and will also pay dividends in the future as discussed in Chapter 9.

2. Protein is helpful. The athlete should remember to eat protein at every meal. [8, 9, 10] If you don't have protein in your system, the muscles can't properly repair themselves.

3. There is evidence that low-carbohydrate diets hasten muscle breakdown. Carbohydrate has a protein-sparing effect so eating sufficient carbohydrates reduces the risk of losing muscle mass along with fat. [11] This is tricky because since your goal is to lose weight, you will be restricting calories but you should still include all of the macronutrients (protein, carbohydrate, fat).

EXPECTING TO LOOK EXCEPTIONAL

The pre-race expo is an eye-popping experience. Fit and fabulous athletes are everywhere and they are dressed for maximum impact. It is intimidating. It is inspiring. But is it attainable?

The average woman is about 26% body fat and she does not look lean. Even in the "athletic" range of body fat (18-22%) women may not look exceptionally fit, especially in a tri outfit. How you will look at your goal weight depends on how you are built and what your genetics dictate about fat distribution. The people that are naturally lean are not reading this book.

Women in the low teens of body fat have some muscle definition and look much leaner than average, but they *still* jiggle. Ladies, if you want to look like Desiree Ficker or Becky Lavelle, you need a miracle. You will also have to be *extremely* lean, right on the edge of unhealthy levels.

Men are more likely driven to lose weight to improve performance rather than appearance. A man of average body fat will not be ripped to shreds with calves like an anatomy lesson and veins popping out everywhere.

Dreaming the dream of looking fast is part of the allure of the sport. Age-grouper Kevin Shaw has come a long way, losing over 100 pounds in 2 years. He is impressed by the professional triathletes, but is realistic about it. "I understand the amount of work and discipline that goes into creating such a great body. Is the super lean look something that you would like to have? I would love to have the look, but I am not willing to make the sacrifices required. I am happy to be healthy and active while enjoying pizza, ice cream and beer. I don't want to make training my life."

Genetics rule how you will look. Arriving at a body composition that is both pleasing (to you), functional and reasonable to maintain is the key to satisfaction and success. As Kevin says, "I will never weigh less than 200 lbs. I've come to terms with that. I am where I am. I'll probably never look like those in the magazines, but I like knowing I can complete the same race as they do (just MUCH slower)."

Don't plan on looking like the athletes in the magazines. "For real people, there is no Photoshop," says author-triathlete Jayne Williams. "Even if we attain our 'ideal'

weight, tone every muscle to its maximum potential, and achieve the cardiovascular efficiency of a shark, our hips will be too wide, our calves too narrow, our feet too flat, our booties too ample, maybe all at the same time. And yet these bodies can walk, dance, swim, climb mountains and ride a bike from Boston to New York. They can jump on a trampoline and do a forward-facing dog pose. The only thing they can't do is look 'perfect'." [12]

Trying to look like someone else is folly. Don't try. Strive to be the best possible version of *you*.

EXPECTING IT TO BE EASY TO MAINTAIN YOUR WEIGHT LOSS

As you near your goal you will chomp at the bit to see how much faster you are. When you reach it, you will feel a long awaited sense of arrival and synchronicity between body and soul. You will be free of the sense of failure that has haunted you. Your slate will be clean and ready for what tomorrow brings.

By the time you reach your goal, you will have practiced the skills and used the tools so many times that they will come naturally to you. They will help you manage your weight for the rest of your life. You will have to continue to use them forever. The plan presented in this book is a plan for life. No foods are excluded. You will learn how to manage all of it.

Is it easy? It is easier than hating yourself for being overweight. It is easier than many hardships that are part of the human condition. Paying attention to food will have to be on your radar every day. You train almost every day. You watch your food every day. It is a manageable challenge.

Weight maintenance will not be a problem. Your fitness, enjoyment of training, goal orientation and passion will hasten your progress. When you reach your goal you will know how to manage food *without the crutch of endless training*. When it comes to maintenance, your athletic habits all but guarantee lifetime success.

EXPECTING THE PROCESS TO BE THE SAME WHETHER YOU ARE MALE OR FEMALE

Men and women differ in their eating patterns, expectations, self-esteem, and ease with weight loss [13]. There is evidence that some people, especially female runners, use calories more efficiently than others [14].

The sexes also respond differently to exercise. A study followed the effect of exercise on formerly sedentary subjects that ate as usual, but added 45 minutes of exercise 5 days per week for 16 months. The participants were evaluated regularly to see how long it would take for body composition to improve. It took the men 9 months to show significant weight and body fat loss. After 16 months, the women showed *no changes* [15]. Women respond poorly to exercise as a means for weight loss.

Part of the reason for the difference in how men and women lose weight lies in the location of their body fat stores. Women tend to store fat in the gluteal-femoral region while men store it the abdominal region. Fat located in the abdominal region (where men have it) is burned more readily than fat in the typical female locations below the waist [11].

Women also have more emotion tied to losing weight and eating behavior. Women eat in response to mood while men seem to eat more in social situations [13]. Eating styles are discussed in Chapter 6.

When it comes to weight loss, men and women are different. Don't get discouraged if your training pals lose weight more easily than you. You will get to where you want to be if you persist.

RACE PHOTOS

Nowhere is the contrast between age-group reality and elite-level fantasy more vividly displayed than in race photos. There was a time when only professional athletes were caught on film during a race. No more. Nowadays, the camera guy is everywhere and smiling, flexing and sucking it in as you go by is *de rigueur*.

Thanks to the internet, photo proofs are displayed online for the world to see. To say that the camera adds weight is an understatement. It adds 10 pounds of floppy, pasty flesh. Many of the photos are so superbly unflattering one must conclude that the photographer is *trying* to take the shot at the worst possible moment; mouths agape, tongues flapping, gut hanging over the shorts, cellulite rippling in all its glory. The array of misshapen forms and unfortunate facial expressions can be depressing if you take them too seriously. You may chuckle at first when you see them, but you may wonder, "Do I *really* look like that?"

We have a fascination with wanting to know how others see us. As unflattering as those photos can be, we can't help but look at them. Unfortunately, they pretty much tell the truth. Ever notice how the photos of your friend look about right, but the ones of you are way off?

Race photos are gasoline on the fire if you are unhappy with your body. Sometimes a dose of reality is what you need to get moving. Welcome to reality. Find your worst photo and make that your "before" photo. With time and effort, your body will improve. If you get lucky, the camera guy will one day capture the sleek speed machine that you have become.

MUSCLES!

Expect to succeed. Losing weight is intoxicating. Despite the hardships, it is thrilling to see your transformation. As you near your weight goal you will see muscles you have never seen before. They have been there all along but when you finally see them, it is fantastic. Don't be embarrassed to look at yourself in the mirror and admire your work. Imprint the new you in your memory.

Women often lose weight in the upper body first so don't be surprised if your shirts get loose before your pants do. Men tend to lose the pot belly first. The parts that hold onto fat will continue to do so, but they will shrink.

Friends will ask "Hey, have you been working out?" as if you have piled on pounds of muscle. Women may ask, "What did you do to tone your arms?" You will snicker to yourself because you finally know that the secret to looking lean is not training to make the muscles bigger, it is losing fat so that the muscles *show*. Body builders have known this all along.

How good will you look? You will see. How fast will you get? You will find out. Getting lean will do more for your race times and your psyche than anything money can buy.

2 How Important Is it to Be Lean?

Looks aren't everything and neither is speed...
but I'd sure like to look like I'm going fast!

There is no set standard of body fat for any sport. It is not the rules, but the demands of the sport itself that dictate the body fat levels of high performing athletes. The body fat percentages reported in triathletes by the United States Olympic Committee are 10-23 % for females, 3-9% for males. Triathletes as a group are very lean and it is rare to see an age-group winner with much to spare.

People that tend to carry weight face an enormous challenge if they want to achieve the body fat levels of a competitive triathlete.

LOW BODY FAT IS IMPORTANT FOR TRIATHLETES

If you were shopping for an ideal triathlete's body, you would choose one with a high VO_2 max (ability to utilize oxygen) and favorable running economy that is generally tall, lean and lightly built [16, 17, 18, 19].

Money can't buy any of these attributes. But with effort you can improve your VO_2 max a little, run better and get leaner. Getting leaner is among the most important attributes of a successful triathlete.

In a 2009 study, triple-ironman athletes were analyzed for body fat percentage, training volume and various body dimensions to determine which characteristics were associated with the fastest finish times. Low body fat was the best predictor of a fast race time. It was more important than any other measurement of body size. It was even more important than training volume [20]. This holds true in shorter triathlon distances as well. Numerous body parameters of elite and junior elite triathletes were measured at the 1987 World Triathlon Championships. Of the components tested, body fat level was the best predictor of an athlete's success [21]. In triathlon, leaner is faster.

HOW MUCH FASTER WILL I GET?

Complicated questions are best answered by experts. Alan Couzens, MS (Sports Science) is an Exercise Physiologist & Coach currently working at Endurance Corner's Human Performance Lab in Boulder, Colorado. As such, he spends his days investigating the physiology of athletes of all shapes and sizes. Alan graciously provided his expertise for this section.

HOW BODY FAT INFLUENCES THE SWIM

Chatard (1985) was one of the first to show that swimmers with more body fat exhibit the lowest energy cost for a given speed [22]. In studies that have examined the differences in economy between male and female swimmers, differences in the vicinity of 30% less energy for a given speed in accordance with a 7-8% increase in body fat have been observed [23, 24].

However, swimming performance (at least over typical short duration swim events) is better correlated with high levels of torque/body size than high levels of economy [25]. Therefore, swimmers should be more concerned with building sufficient muscle to achieve competitive race torques, while triathletes should be concerned with achieving an optimal amount of muscle that allows them to produce 'decent' levels of torque (and corresponding stroke lengths) in the water, without adding excessive muscle mass that will be detrimental on the run.

Additionally, differences in technical competence can account for more than 50% of the differences in swimming economy [26]. Therefore, a focus on technical competence can afford a better 'bang for your buck' for the time-limited triathlete than attempting to radically change your body type.

HOW BODY FAT INFLUENCES CYCLING

Hilly courses
For a given athlete on a 4% grade (a pretty typically encountered grade in rolling and hilly triathlons), dropping body weight offers the following speed benefit for a given wattage of 200W [27].

160 lb triathlete @ 200W up a 4% grade = 10.5 mph

180 lb triathlete @ 200W up a 4% grade = 9.8 mph

200 lb triathlete @ 200W up a 4% grade = 8.8 mph

However, this pre-supposes that no 'watts are lost' in the weight-loss process, in other words that optimal muscle mass is maintained. This deserves more than mere lip service, as it is common for adult athletes to adopt a 'weight loss' focus over a 'muscle gain' focus. The paths of Lance Armstrong and Miguel Indurain are relatively common among the crème de la crème of elite road cyclists, i.e. an early focus on developing a big strong engine and a later focus on slimming down the chassis.

Flat courses
Flat courses offer relatively less benefit to a lighter athlete than hilly courses [28, 29]. While performance in climbing is closely related to watts per kilogram, performance on the flat is more closely correlated with watts per kilo^0.32 [27, 28]. In other words, a light body weight is ~2/3 less important on the flat than when going uphill. This is because, while a smaller athlete usually has a lower frontal area and therefore less drag, this does not compensate for the benefits of the bigger engine that sits in a larger athlete's drag shadow while riding on the flat.

It should also be mentioned that this scaling assumes a 'typical' mass:frontal area relationship. If a tall, skinny athlete loses bodyweight, this is not likely to have any sizable impact on frontal area, but if muscle is lost it IS likely to have a significant impact on the athlete's ability to create power.

The greatest impact of weight loss on flat cycling is going to be found in decreased rolling resistance. This is going to have the greatest impact at low cycling speeds and in non-aerodynamic positions, where rolling resistance dominates aerodynamic resistance. This situation, hopefully, represents the complete opposite of your current racing situation. Specifically, at speeds of 4.5-7 miles per hour, a decrease in bodyweight of 20 lbs for a 200 lb athlete will result in a 5-8% lower power output on the flat. However, at more typical race speeds of 24 mph, the benefit is reduced to 1.25-2% less power for a given speed [30].

HOW BODY FAT INFLUENCES RUNNING

Within a given sample, the relationship between energy cost and speed is almost linearly related to body weight, with good runners exhibiting an oxygen cost of approximately 200 ml of oxygen per kilometer traveled per kilogram of bodyweight. Therefore, according to this model, a reduction in bodyweight from 200 lbs to 180 lbs (~9 kg of bodyweight) will result in a decreased O2 cost of 1.8L of O2 per kilometer. At a fixed VO2 output of say, 4L/min, this represents a difference in pace of ~45s/mile (6:33/mi for the 180 pounder vs. 7:16/mi for the 200 lb runner). Assuming economy is constant, this ~10% difference with a 10% reduction in bodyweight stays constant across various race paces.

However, the big picture is not quite as simple as it seems because changes in body composition will result in changes in both economy and also (arguably) VO_2 max. With athletes with more (oxidative) leg muscle exhibiting the best economy and runners with either too much fat relative to muscle (endomorphs) or too much bone relative to muscle (ectomorphs) exhibiting poorer economy numbers than an athlete with appropriate body composition (for running: ecto-mesomorphs). For this reason, it is important to identify an optimal body composition that results in the best economy for an individual athlete's frame.

For instance, at the extreme, a 6'4" super skinny 150 lb runner with 35 lbs of muscle will likely have similar economy numbers to a 5'0", 150 lb overweight runner with 35 lbs of muscle, and both will be well above the 200 ml/kg/km figure of 'good' runners. In order to get there, the taller athlete will need to gain muscle, while the shorter will need to lose fat, despite identical starting weights.

© marvellousworld/fotolia.com

THE BOTTOM LINE: RACE TIME COMPARISONS

Table 1 and Table 2 below illustrate likely influences of body fat reduction on 2 different athletes. They are overly-simplified and can't possibly take into account all of the variables that influence performance. Keep the following in mind as you read them:

- Swim: Any time 'lost' with increased drag due to decreased buoyancy in the water can easily be made up for (for anyone but elite swimmers) in technique improvement.
- Bike: These times represent a completely flat course. If any hills are present, the improvements with fat reduction are magnified.
- Run: These are purely 'mechanical' improvements. Improvements in thermo-regulation with decreased body fat will lead to even greater improvements on warm courses.
- Overall: Particularly for the Ironman, the shorter the race duration gets, the higher the intensity it can be raced at. Therefore, there will be additional improvement coming from the fact that the race is going from a 15 hr effort to a 14 hr effort with no energy increase.

Table 1 *Comparison of race times as male athlete age 30 reduces body fat*

Ironman Distance	Overweight 200 lbs. BF 26 %	Fit 180 lbs. BF 16%	Triathlete 160 lbs. BF 6%
Swim Time	1:25	1:33	1:41
Bike Time (flat)	7:00	6:50	6:42
Run Time	6:15	5:38	5:01
	15:10 (w/30 min T)	14:31 (w/30 min T)	13:54 (w/30 min T)

Table 2 *Comparison of race times as female athlete age 40 reduces body fat*

Olympic Distance	Overweight 180 lbs. BF 32%	Fit BF 162 lbs. 22%	Triathlete 144 lbs. BF 12%
Swim Time	00:35	00:39	00:42
Bike Time (flat)	1:15	1:14	1:13
Run Time	1:20	1:12	1:04
	3:25 (w/15 min T)	3:20 (w/15 min T)	3:14 (w/15 min T)

BODY FAT AND HEAT

Body fat is a terrific insulator. It may be helpful in cold weather, but it is a hindrance especially in hot and humid environments. Heat production is directly proportional to exercise intensity. If your goal is to move at a comfortable pace, you will be able to manage, but if your goal is to be fast, you will train and race at the upper limits of intensity. When intensity increases, so does your body temperature. Once you go above 38-40°C (100.4-104°F), your brain signals a systemic shutdown forcing you to slow down so that the body can cool off (and stay alive). Athletes with higher levels of body fat reach this upper temperature limit more quickly than leaner ones [31].

Getting lean will diminish your tendency to retain heat and will help you perform better in hot and humid conditions [30, 31].

PICK THE RIGHT RACE

You can see how important it is to pick the right race if you want to minimize the negative impact of extra body fat. If doing relatively well in your age-group matters, pick a course with a cold swim, a flat ride and cool weather.

3 Where Do You Stand?

It's simple, if it jiggles, it is fat.

– Arnold Schwarzenegger

BODY BUILD

The three components of body build are frame size, body type and body composition. Each component of body build has a role in your potential as an athlete and in your appearance.

You can't change the size of your skeleton (frame size). Body type can't be changed either, but understanding the various types will help you formulate a realistic goal (see Figure 1).

Body Composition is where the action is. Training and diet can profoundly influence the ratio of lean mass to fat mass in any body type.

Figure 1 *Summary of Body Types*

Body Type

There are three body types but no one is purely of one type. We are all combinations of the three. The process of determining body type is known as somatotyping. The brawny football player-types that populate the Clydesdale divisions have predominantly endomorphic characteristics and pro triathletes are mostly ectomorphic. No amount of training or diet manipulation will transform one body type into another. The best you can do is become a lean, strong and fit version of yourself.

Endomorph

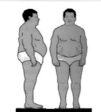

- Stocky, pear shaped body, short arms and legs
- Wide hips and shoulders
- Wider front to back rather than side to side
- A lot of fat on the body, upper arms and thighs
- Gains muscle and fat easily
- Has hard time with agility, speed and sustained running but has high lung capacity

Mesomorph

- A wedge shaped body
- Wide broad shoulders, narrow hips
- Muscled arms and legs
- Narrow from front to back rather than side to side
- Minimum amount of fat, can lose weight easily
- Excels in strength, agility & speed sports

Ectomorph

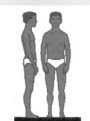

- Receding chin
- Narrow shoulders and hips
- A narrow chest and abdomen
- Thin arms and legs
- Little muscle and fat, easily gets lean and hard looking
- Excels at endurance sports and gymnastics
- Superior thermoregulation

Source: http://www.brianmac.co.uk

© fotolia.com

BODY COMPOSITION

WHAT IS LEAN MASS?

You hear the terms *body fat, BMI,* and *lean mass* thrown around but do you know what they mean? Body fat is pretty clear, it is the number of pounds of fat on your body, usually expressed as a percentage of total body weight. Triathletes want the body fat number to be low because extra fat is metabolically inactive tissue that does not contribute to performance, it just has to be carried around. Carrying extra fat is a real disadvantage in running and uphill cycling, both activities which require the athlete to tangle with gravity.

Lean mass is more interesting. Lean mass is everything other than fat. It is not just muscle. Lean mass is also your organs and your skeleton. Your bones account for about 14% of total body weight [32]. What you may not realize is that stomach contents and even water are counted as lean mass. That is why it is important to get tested under the same circumstances each time. If you get tested after a meal, the numbers will be different than after an overnight fast. A training session can dehydrate you a little, which will also influence results. Drinking a big glass of water before testing does more than increase your weight a few ounces, the water will be counted as lean mass. The differences do not reflect changes in the amount of muscle you have, but of the other components of lean body mass.

BMI doesn't tell an athlete much about the composition of the body. It is discussed at the end of the chapter.

STICK WITH ONE METHOD

It is important to choose a method of body composition analysis, a device or a particular testing facility that you can stick with for a few years. If you jump around there will be a lot of variation in your data and it will be harder to see progress. There is a margin of error in every type of analysis, but it is smaller in some methods than in others. Pick an accurate method.

If losing fat is important to you, take care to get *helpful* results. Helpful results will show how and if your body composition has changed. You can not gauge this properly if you compare results of a skinfold with results from a handheld device. Athletes that do this have no way of knowing which results are accurate and more importantly, they can not tell if their fat loss efforts have been effective. Getting a surprisingly high body fat reading from a portable device at a race expo can ruin your day and your race if you take it too seriously. Why put yourself through that? Persevere with one method until you reach your goal.

MEASURING METHODS

BIOIMPEDANCE DEVICES

One of most common and widely available methods for measuring body fat is with bioimpedance devices. These devices include portable hand-held versions, special bathroom scales and machines that are used in a clinical setting at a doctor's office.

Handheld

Handheld devices pass an electric current from one hand, through the body, to the other hand. Health clubs and race expos often use these devices because they are portable and easy to use [33].

Measurements from these devices are not very accurate. They tend under-estimate lean body mass by 2.3-5.6 kg (5.06-12.32 lbs) and to underestimate fat mass even more [33].

These devices are not a good way to determine how much of your body weight is lean mass and how much is fat. You can, however, use them to compare readings over time to see if there is a trend in one direction or another.

Home Scales

Home body fat scales measure electrical current from one foot to the other, but they lack input from the torso. The computer inside the scale uses a formula to estimate the torso numbers then combines it with the measurement from the lower body to determine the result displayed on the scale. Studies have compared results with people of different body shapes using these scales. The scales are fairly accurate in women with a pear shaped body, but the accuracy is very poor in women with an apple shaped body and for men [34].

Tanita scales has overcome this issue by adding handles to some models. The user can measure the body composition of the upper body by using the handles and the lower body composition by standing on the scale, using the foot sensors. One can even measure composition of each limb which can be important when trying to overcome an injury or strength/mass imbalance between limbs.

Body water is also displayed on some scales. Body water is simply hydration. An athlete should be able to tell the difference between dehydration and fat loss with one of these scales.

Testing in a Clinic

When testing is done in a doctor's office using bioimpedance, the athlete lies down and electrodes are placed on a hand and foot. A current is then passed through the entire body. One of the main advantages of this method is that the testing is done by trained personnel under standard conditions [35]. When done this way, the results are quite accurate.

DISPLACEMENT METHODS

The Bod Pod

Measuring body composition by Air Displacement plethysmography has become popular with the introduction of the BOD POD® Body Composition Tracking System (see Figure 2). It has taken some time, but since its introduction in 1994, this device has become widely available in athletic testing and training facilities, gyms and even some health food stores.

The BOD POD® measures the volume of the athlete's body as he sits in a small fiberglass chamber. The body's volume is the amount of air displaced by the athlete when he gets into the chamber. By breathing into an air circuit, the amount of air in the lungs is subtracted and true body volume is calculated.

Figure 2 *The Bod Pod*

photo provided by Life Measurement, Inc.

This method provides consistent readings but it tends to underreport absolute percentages of body fat [36]. One of the advantages of this method is that it requires little of the technician doing the measuring so repeated measures over time are likely to be consistent.

Hydrostatic weighing

Hydrostatic weighing, also known as underwater weighing, works by comparing dry land weight with the weight while submerged in a tank of water. Body density is estimated from the difference of the two weights and then a formula is used to calculate the amount of body fat and thus, body fat percentage.

This method is highly accurate but not particularly conven-ient. It is time-consuming and requires a large specialized tank. Subjects must get wet and hold their breath for 10-20 seconds.

SKINFOLD ANALYSIS

Skinfold measurement is among the most accurate methods of assessing body composition. It is well worth the embarrassment of having someone grab and measure your fat.

This method uses various formulas and tables which are based upon the number and location of skinfolds tested. Testing can be done at 3, 4 or 7 locations. The measurements are based upon the relationship between subcutaneous fat which is under your skin, and visceral fat which is internal, between your organs.

Skinfold testing should be done by a trained clinician. The skin should be measured within 2 seconds of pinching and ideally, measurements should be taken by the same person each time you are tested. In any case, returning to the same facility makes it more likely that the technicians have been trained to follow the same protocol.

This method has had some accuracy problems in the past because the formulas to convert skinfold measurements into body fat percentages did not work very well in Hispanic and African-American men and women; they require different conversion formulas because of differences in body structure [37, 38].

The New Zealand Triathlon Academy uses the skinfolds alone, without applying any formulas. This method does not give body composition percentages, but it accounts for changes up or down. Current criteria for the sum of 8 skinfolds for Academy triathletes are 35-75 mm for males and 45-100 mm for females [39].

Do it yourself?

Home calipers are widely available and are useful for triathletes that want to see if they are getting leaner or not. They have some advantages over a bioimpedance device in that they do not require batteries and do not involve electronics that may be sensitive to floor surfaces and moisture. Up to 4 skinfold sites can be used. The measurements can be compared to a chart or used in an online calculator to estimate body fat percentage, but the results are not very accurate.

IMAGING TECHNOLOGIES

X-ray and MRIs can be used to measure the size and location of fatty tissue, estimate bone density and lean body mass. These technologies are expensive and time-consuming and at this point, not used much for athletes interested in body composition analysis. They are extremely accurate.

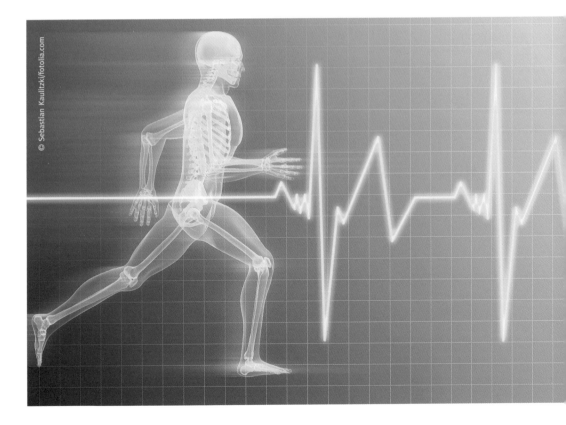

© Sebastian Kaulitzki/fotolia.com

FACTORS THAT INFLUENCE RESULTS

Many factors can influence body composition results. Check with the facility beforehand to find out what to wear, and how to best time eating, drinking and training to optimize results. Write the protocol down so you can repeat it precisely each time you are tested. Here is a list of some of the things that can influence results [40, 41, 42].

1. Hydration status – liquids and alcohol consumed within 24 hours of testing

2. Dampness/sweat on skin

3. Body temperature

4. Time since your last training session

5. Ethnicity

6. Gender

7. Age

8. Level of adiposity

9. Competence of person performing the test

10. Reliability of the computer model and formulas used to calculate results

11. Medications in your system that influence hydration or inflammation

HOW TO USE THE RESULTS

Body composition information is most important when you are setting goals or want to see how your body has responded to a particular training or diet regime.

When you have your body composition analyzed, get as much data as you can from the technician. Sometimes you are given only the body fat %. Ideally, you will receive a written report with all sorts of data such as total lean body mass, total fat body mass, total body weight and if applicable, skinfold measurements.

Chapter 4 describes how to calculate weight loss goals based on body composition data.

USE YOUR HOME SCALE, TOO

Weigh yourself at home as soon as you are done with your body composition test. Compare your weight on your home scale with the one at the testing center and make note if there is a difference. Now you know how much you weigh at a given percentage of body fat and you can use the scale to follow your weight loss progress. Have your body composition re-tested at least every 6 months.

THE BODY CHECK

Can you imagine there was a time when the only method commonly used to evaluate fatness was the good-ole eyeball? Even in this age of high technology, the eyes are among the finest instruments. The only problem is that you can't see your backside very well.

Once you reach your goal, spend some time looking at yourself. You will look so darn good it will be a pleasure, but that is not why you are looking. Take in the details. Create a new vision of "normal" in your mind. Notice the striations on that muscle when you are lean? When you sit down, pull up your shirt and study your belly, what do you see? Memorize the details. In the future you can use your eyes to tell you are putting on fat.

LIMITATIONS OF THE BODY MASS INDEX

The Body Mass Index (BMI) was designed as a simple tool to help evaluate an individual's risk for particular diseases such as stroke, hypertension, certain cancers, etc. The BMI does not tell you much about how you are built or what proportion of your body weight is lean mass (bone, muscle, organs) and how much is fat. Two individuals may have identical BMI numbers but vastly different body fat levels. Table 3 illustrates this point. Charts and online calculators are widely available and they make it simple to determine your BMI. All you need to know is your height and weight.

Weight management programs use BMI as a basis for determining goal weights for clients, but the BMI doesn't give triathletes what they need to know in order to improve body composition.

Table 3 *Comparison of body composition measures of two men with same BMI*

Subjects	BMI	% Body Fat	Total Fat Weight	Total Lean Weight
Tom is 5'0" and weighs 128 lbs	25	6.25 %	8 lbs	120 lbs
Joe is 6'0" and weighs 186 lbs	25	14%	26 lbs	160 lbs

The athletes in Table 3 illustrate the limitations of BMI as a measure of body composition. While both athletes are in the healthy weight range, there is a large difference between their body fat levels.

4 Three Goals

Swim, Bike, Run.
Lose, Maintain, Stabilize.

Getting to the end of the weight management rainbow requires that you accomplish 3 goals:

1. Lose: Setting a weight goal and reaching it is the first step in tackling your weight problem. When you reach this weight you will look and perform better than ever. Call it the "Better Than Ever" number.

2. Maintain: Goal number two is holding onto (within 2 pounds) your Better Than Ever weight for 6 consecutive weeks as you transition from losing weight to maintaining it. If you go above the 2 pound cushion, you have to start the 6 weeks again.

3. Stabilize: The third goal is to have your body composition analyzed (again) and to replace your Better Than Ever number with a body fat range that you can live with for the long term and translating that into your new, "normal weight range."

THE FIRST GOAL (LOSE)

How do you set the right goal? What is your Better Than Ever weight? Have a body composition analysis and consider the factors discussed in this chapter. Use the information to come up with a number that will make you look, feel and perform better than ever.

CONSIDER WHAT IS IDEAL FOR THE SPORT

Triathletes strive for a combination of three body type ideals: swimming necessitates buoyancy (requiring some body fat), runners desire no excess weight, and cyclists strive for strength and stamina [43]. If optimal performance is driving your quest for leanness, it is likely that leaner is better, within reason. Consider the body fat percentages of high level triathletes as set forth in Table 4.

Table 4 *Body fat % of high level athletes [44, 45]*

Body fat %	Female range%	Male range%
Swimming	14-24	7-12
Cycling	12-18	8-10
Running	10-19	6-13
Triathlon	10-23	3-9

The Body fat values in Table 4 are given as a range is because individuals vary. Not every male athlete will achieve his best performance at 8% body fat. Some will reach lower values and still improve performance, while others will find it impossible to get down that low and will have to compete at a higher value [46]. Women should not strive for single-digit body fat levels because it is unhealthy [11].

Do you know how your own performances vary with body composition or weight? Some athletes have kept track of this information all along. Those are the ones who aren't reading this chapter because they already know what their goals are. If you want to start collecting data, use the chart in Appendix A to track your own race performances. In time you will discover what is optimum.

Consider your athletic history. What did you weigh when you performed well as an adult athlete? Use that as a starting point, but don't stop there.

CONSIDER WHO YOU ARE

Don't look too far back

As long as we are talking about history, it may tempting to set your Better Than Ever goal as your weight in high school or at some other time when you were fit and healthy. That number may be emotionally powerful for you, but consider carefully whether it is right for you now:

- You probably have tried to get back to that number many times in your life so it is connected with past failures. Does that more strongly compel you to reach it or does it open a troubling can of worms?

- Were you a triathlete back then? Your goal should reflect your identity as an adult athlete, not as the kid you used to be.

- Have you had children? Sorry, but that changes your body forever. Don't use numbers that pre-date childbirth.

- Have you been building muscle in the gym? Chances are you want to hang on to it. As Kevin says, "The top Ironman athletes begin to look 'marathon-ish,' and that's not the look I want. I love to lift weights so I'll never be that small and in reality, my body seems to like the weight I'm at."

  Likewise, if you have put on significant weight since your youth, you have also gained muscle (to move your bigger body around). It may not be possible to get back to that old weight without getting rid of muscle.

- Are you nearing 50 or beyond? Higher body fat is an unavoidable consequence of age. The number that worked for you in your 20's and 30's is not going to work in your 50's, 60's or 70's.

If a number from your past is no longer suitable, find a new one, *a better one*.

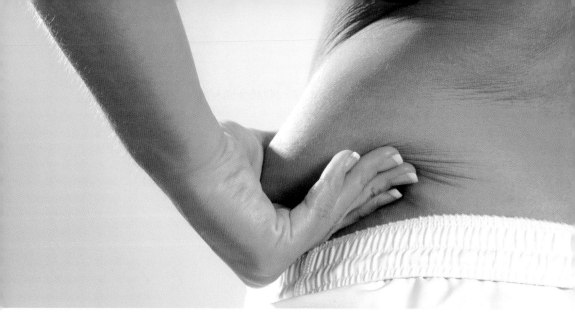

CONSIDER THE SKIN YOU'RE IN

When you lose weight, your body shrinks and it can take some time for your skin to catch up. If you are over 40, it may never shrink back and you will have to choose between being lean and wrinkly, or chubby and smooth. In some cases, cosmetic surgery is the only way to get rid of the excess (see Chapter 16). Triathlete Anna put it this way, "If I lose too much weight I look like a skin suit on a coat hanger. I can't go below 160 before my skin hangs off of me and my breasts disappear."

If you have loose skin or are getting older, you may look better with a few more pounds. If you are all about performance, let your skin flap wildly but get as lean as you can.

CONSIDER YOUR BODY COMPOSITION

It would be nice to know how lean your favorite triathlete is; then you could just pick that number as your goal. But could you? Not really. Body fat looks different on different people. What is attractive on one person may not look work so well for another.

The worksheet in Appendix B will help you determine what your body fat % will be at various weights (based on current body composition data). If the Better Than Ever number you have in mind is on the high end of the body fat range of successful triathletes (see Table 4) it is probably a good number.

CONSIDER WEIGHT FLUCTUATIONS AND MAINTENANCE

Your weight probably fluctuates a few pounds from day to day. When setting your goal, allow for those fluctuations. One way to do this is to decide your goal will be a range rather than a single number. This will become more important when you are working on maintaining your weight for 6 weeks (goal two). There is no merit to choosing a rock-bottom number that you can not possibly maintain. Your aim is to choose a number that you are so happy with, that you are willing to change the way you eat forever to hold onto it.

STICK WITH YOUR BETTER THAN EVER NUMBER UNTIL YOU REACH IT

Achieving a particular weight is the first step in the process but in the long run, the number itself is only a symbol of success. The purpose of the number is to give you a lofty, motivating goal.

In lifetime weight management, achieving a goal weight is a victory that will set other victories in motion. Reaching it will change how you see yourself. It may be tempting to modify your goal along the way, but don't. There is danger in doing so.

When you are working very hard to achieve a formidable goal, your psyche directs exceptional resources to the endeavor. These resources include dreams, motivation, fantasy, patience and a little fear as well. Getting to your Better Than Ever number has to be a gigantic goal, like reaching the Ironman finish line. You must invest so much into it that you will not tolerate failure. That is also why choosing the right Better Than Ever number (and the right Ironman race) is so important.

If you were doing an Ironman race, and 5 miles from the finish you decided it was no longer a worthy goal *and you quit*, how would you feel the next day? How would you feel about that choice for years to come? "Pain is temporary. Pride is forever." applies to more than races, it applies to reaching your weight goal too. Reaching your goal is every bit as important for your sense of self-worth and power as an Ironman finish line is.

Your Better Than Ever goal is your Ironman Finish. You must not fail!

THE SECOND GOAL (MAINTAIN)

MAINTAIN YOUR BETTER THAN EVER WEIGHT FOR SIX WEEKS

Once you have reached your Better Than Ever weight, you will move to the second goal and maintain it for 6 weeks. Celebrate your accomplishment and bask in your success. Buy some new clothes. Go running without a shirt. Wear your short-shorts.

Continue to do all of the things you did to reach your goal. Keep following your plan, keep applying the 3 skills and keep using the tools that have been helpful along the way. As you will shift from losing weight to maintaining it, you can begin to eat a little more. Add up to 200 calories to your daily target. If your weight stays the same, you have reached your new normal calorie intake. If you continue to lose weight, go ahead and add another 200 calories a day and so on, until your weight stabilizes. Watch your weight carefully. For all intents and purposes, you have arrived at your new lifelong calorie target.

If you creep above your goal weight, you will have to redouble your efforts to get back down and hold it for 6 *more* weeks. It is alright if you lose a little more weight during maintenance; just don't let it creep more than 2 pounds above your Better Than Ever number.

Increase your training volume and intensity as you wish. The additional calorie burn will help you keep your weight stable as you increase your intake. Step up your training to desired levels and by all means, enter a race and test out the new machine. See how it feels.

THE THIRD GOAL (STABILIZE)

DEFINE YOUR NEW NORMAL WEIGHT

The third goal is to define your (new) normal weight:
1. Base it on the body composition data you obtain following 6 weeks of maintenance.
2. Consider how difficult it was to maintain your Better Than Ever weight.
3. Add 3-5 pounds so that you have a range of normal weight that you never go above.

It is important to sustain your Better Than Ever weight for at least 6 weeks *before* you re-test your body composition. In those weeks, you can return to performance level training and hopefully you will be spending time in the gym. You will probably have lost some lean mass during your weight loss period and you will be eating more to accommodate the added training volume.

All of these changes will affect your body. They should stimulate some muscle growth. With new muscle and much less fat, the old data won't be correct anymore. Body composition can change several percentage points during a season so testing will be an ongoing process that you repeat at least every 6 months.

WHAT WILL YOUR LIFETIME BODY FAT PERCENTAGE BE?

As described above, your body composition data will allow you to formulate a new normal weight. This weight will represent a certain body fat level, but you will continue using the scale to monitor your weight between body fat tests.

- Give yourself some leeway. If it was difficult to stay at your goal number for 6 weeks, can you maintain a few pounds above it with relative ease? One or two pounds will probably not make much difference in the long run and if your body weight is easier to maintain there, consider using that number as your new goal. Better yet, give yourself a 5 pound range of acceptable weight. Monitor it carefully and if your weight goes above the range, immediately go back to the calorie target that worked for you. The sooner you jump on the weigh gain, the easier it will come off. This is the prime benefit of weighing yourself every day and knowing how your weight fluctuates. You will know immediately when you need to nip weight gain in the bud. Expect to dust off your calorie target a few times a year.

- You may discover that you don't perform well at your goal weight. Use the worksheet in Appendix A to compare your race/training performances. You should be faster, especially running. If you aren't, evaluate your body fat %. Maybe you have gone too far. Allow your weight to go up a few pounds then re-evaluate.

- You may not like your new looks. Maybe you are too bony or lack power on the bike. Maybe your arms look too skinny. In time you will regain the muscle you lost. Continue to train and allow yourself to move off the Better Than Ever number a little. You may find that in time your body adjusts and you are happy at a slightly higher weight.

- Don't judge success on how good you look in tri-clothes. Triathlon clothes are unforgiving to say the least. Clothes with 'compression' and 'support' are popular but they are double-edged swords; the skin that is being compressed has to go somewhere so it balloons out over waistbands and leg grippers, making you look more like a sausage than an endurance machine. This does not mean you are fat. It is a skin-compression thing. Having worked hard to look great, you should not tolerate clothing that makes you look bad. Spend the time and money to look awesome. You deserve it.

- In the months and years to come, your weight may fluctuate 10 pounds even though you maintain the same body fat levels. If you seem to be putting on weight and returning to your calorie target does not take it away, don't despair, it is time for another body composition test. Perhaps you have put on some muscle.

USE THE SCALE

As wonderful as body composition testing can be, it is impractical to have it done every day. The handheld devices and scales aren't accurate enough to replace a thorough analysis and it is important for various reasons to weigh yourself often (see Chapter 8). There is no escaping the scale.

If you synchronize your scale with your body fat data (e.g. at 140 lbs I am 22% body fat) you can use the scale to track your progress on a daily basis, then have your body composition retested every few months and make adjustments as needed. The scale is not your enemy, it is just a tool.

THE MIRACLE OF YOUR STABLE WEIGHT

At some point in the future, you will have used the 3 skills and the tools (discussed later) for so long they will become "normal" eating. When you are eating well without starving, you are able to train and race and your weight is stable, you will have reached the happy place known as a healthy, stable weight. Have you ever achieved that before? It is an astonishing place.

At this weight there is no room to create a calorie deficit by eliminating high calorie density foods because you are already applying the 3 skills. You are already doing everything right.

This is the point of acceptance because *you will know* that there is nothing else you can do to *maintain* a leaner body (you could get leaner for a few weeks to prepare for a race, but you would not be able to hold it for long). This is the point when you can look happily in the mirror and realize...

THIS IS IT.

What is miraculous about this stage is that you can finally truly accept yourself; perhaps for the first time in your life. You can say without cringing, "I have big thighs," or "I can't see my six pack abs but I know they are there," and you don't have to follow with, "I will have to eat better and lose 10 pounds." You will have already done everything and you will have no regrets, make no apologies and can get on with the business of being a tremendous athlete and an inspiration to those around you. You can look in the mirror and say with conviction, "what a stud!"

PART 3 – MANAGING FOOD

5 Your Calorie Target

Triathletes thrive in defined spaces:
miles, hours, zones, watts and calories.

YOU NEED A CALORIE TARGET

Changing your weight is a matter of manipulating calorie intake and expenditure. To gain weight, you need to take more calories in than you expend. To lose weight, you must create a calorie deficit. If math was all there was to it, you wouldn't be reading this book. We will soon discuss how to manage food so that you can live happily in a state of calorie-deprivation. For now, let's talk about what the numbers mean.

Calories in – calories out = net energy balance

Your calorie target is the number of calories you will eat each day to create a calorie deficit that will get you to your weight loss goal in a reasonable amount of time. If you create a deficit that is too large, you will put your body and mind into a state of starvation which is counter-productive. Your metabolism will slow down, you will lose more muscle than necessary and you will set yourself up, psychologically, for failure. If the calorie deficit is too small, you will not lose weight fast enough to see progress. A reasonable rate of weight loss is 1-2 pounds per week.

All of the food-tracking methods in this book are based on controlling calorie intake (calories in) through one means or another.

CALORIES OUT

Everything you eat has an energy value which is expressed in calories. Your body uses calories in 3 ways:

1. Digestion: The energy needed to digest, metabolize, absorb and store food is known as the thermic effect of food and accounts for about 10% of daily calorie expenditure. Although this process is not something you can control, there is evidence that trained athletes use significantly more energy in these processes than untrained individuals [47].

2. Activity: This is the only component of calorie use that is directly within your control. It can account for 30-80% of the calories expended each day. It includes training and everything else you do during the day. Since activity levels vary from person to person, these calories are accounted for as an overall activity level or activity by activity, using charts and formulas (see Appendix C).

Another way to monitor calorie expenditure is with a Bodybugg®. This device is a combination pedometer-accelerometer (which tracks body movements), heat and moisture sensor on an arm-band (to evaluate exertion levels) that provides readings of calorie expenditure throughout the day and in a 24-hour period.

The display can be worn on the wrist or clipped to your clothing. The data can be downloaded and web-based software provides detailed information. If you use the food tracking program, you can go one step further and see ongoing calorie deficit and surplus. The manufacturer claims the data is 90% accurate over a 24 hour period.

3. Metabolism: The *largest* amount of energy is used to keep your body processes going. Known as the resting metabolic rate (RMR), this is the number of calories your body uses in a 24-hour period while at rest. Accounting for 60-70% of calories used each day, it is influenced by age, lean body mass, gender and genetics. Increasing your muscle mass raises the metabolic rate.

HOW TO FIND YOUR CALORIE TARGET

Assuming you are training about 6 hours per week, most women will lose weight on 1400 calories and most men will lose on 2000 calories a day. These numbers are imprecise shortcuts, but if you can't stand the idea of doing the math, they offer a reasonable starting point.

For a more precise calculation, use the formulas or websites listed in Appendix C or an online calculator. Some of the online calculators account for activity level and some do not. As a rule of thumb, the more information you put into an online calculator, the more precise the result will be.

MATH ISN'T EVERYTHING

No matter what label is used, every weight-loss plan is based on eating fewer calories. Combining nutrients into various combinations may have a role in managing appetite but the net effect is that you are consuming fewer calories. That is not to say that calories are all there is to weight-loss. Indeed, calorie deficits don't predict rates of weight loss very well, especially in the short term. Several factors are responsible, including:

1. Resting metabolic rate slows when the body detects a calorie shortage. The number of calories burned in your daily activities may actually go down because you are *unconsciously* moving less.

2. There is a tendency to under-report food intake [48].

3. Daily weight fluctuations from 2-7 pounds can make it difficult to determine if you have lost weight or not.

4. Calorie expenditure calculations are usually based on the general population and may not take gender or body mass into account. There is also some variation in how efficiently each of us burns calories.

5. The body doesn't respond noticeably to slight calorie deficits. The process of weight loss seems to require a large initial calorie deficit (about 3500 calories in 4-5 days) to get started. Once it begins, the body continues to respond as long as the shortfall is at least 3500 calories per week.

Calorie deficits are fairly accurate predictors of weight loss in the long term (several weeks). Using calories to predict weight loss isn't perfect, but it is the best thing out there. Understanding the limitations should keep you from getting discouraged. The next chapter describes several ways to keep track of calorie intake.

6 Keeping Track

It's not enough that we do our best;
sometimes we have to do what's required.

— Sir Winston Churchill (1874-1965)

The mechanics of losing weight are simple; take in less energy than you expend. The way you go about it, however, must fit your personality and your eating style. Some people love to keep track of every bite and others detest the notion. Identifying your eating style will help you choose a tracking method you can stick with.

WHAT KIND OF EATER ARE YOU?

There are 5 types of eaters. You may fall into one of these categories, or several of them at various times. The first 3 categories: Emotional Eaters, Hungry Meat Eaters and Grazers, are based upon experience and loosely upon scientific research [49]. The other 2 categories are athletes that want to lose about 5 pounds and those that are training for an Ironman event.

EMOTIONAL EATERS

Some people eat more when they are stressed. In scientific circles these are "restrained" and "emotional" eaters. These people are always on a diet, and are very focused on eating the right food.

Emotional Eaters eat to cope with emotions of all kinds; to celebrate victories, to escape frustration and to nurture themselves. They use food as a tranquilizer. Emotional Eaters prefer to eat alone or will eat more when they are alone than when they are with others. They are often, but not always, women.

Emotional Eaters are preoccupied with food and tend to ignore hunger signals. They have trouble with forbidden "trigger" foods. Most of the time, they eat according to a calorie allowance, but these periods of excessive control (being "good") are derailed easily by a violation of the "rules". Rather than accepting an occasional misstep and moving on, restrained eaters go overboard and start eating out of control. Researchers Janet Polivy and Peter Herman call this the "What the Hell" effect [50]. These out of control periods come often enough to counteract the periods of calorie restriction so the athlete never loses weight.

The cycles of controlled vs. out of control eating can occur every few days or weeks. Night eaters go through the cycle every day, waking each morning with guilt and new resolve and by nighttime they have abandoned the fight.

The tools that are most effective for this kind of eater are those that minimize stress. Keeping track of everything they eat gives them a sense of order and control.

In the long run, such an eater benefits from eating within guidelines instead of absolute rules. If there are no rules to "violate," the eater will not so easily be thrown into her "What the Hell" mode. All of the tracking methods are suitable for Emotional Eaters.

HUNGRY MEAT-EATERS

Hungry Meat-Eaters crave fast food and are often men [51]. Also known as "meat and potatoes" types, they want "real" food that is cooked and served hot as a meal at the table. They passively munch on high fat foods like chips and dips, pizza and the like.

Hungry Meat-Eaters prefer high fat foods and are genetically distinct from those that that prefer high carbohydrate foods [52]. They seem to experience hunger more strongly than others. They rate their own hunger signals more strongly than the high carbohydrate eaters rate theirs [51]. They are also known as "unrestrained" eaters. They overeat, but they don't worry about it much.

They eat when desired food is available, whether they are hungry or not. At times they lose control because of hunger and temptation, rather than for emotional reasons.

Hungry Meat-Eaters don't like to write things down or to count calories. They do well with visual systems like the "Visual Plate" or lists like "Clean Food" and benefit from applying the skills discussed in Chapter 7 that steer them to low fat (low calorie density) foods.

GRAZERS

Grazers eat too often. They eat constantly without paying enough attention to total calorie intake. They favor carbohydrates. They are not so much hungry as they are in the habit of munching all the time. If high-calorie treats are around, they will munch it a little at a time until it is gone. Endurance athletes learn to become grazers by necessity. A snack before an early swim, a quick breakfast, midmorning snack, lunch, refuel after training, mid-afternoon snack, dinner, etc.

Grazers can reduce their intake significantly by putting some time between meals and becoming more conscious of their total intake. They would benefit from fewer snack foods and eating a larger variety of healthy foods. The "Visual Plate" and "Clean Food" methods encourage this sort of eating.

FIVE POUNDERS

Athletes that only want to lose about 5 pounds are already lean and healthy, but either they want to shave a few pounds to get to race weight, or they want to reduce their normal weight just a notch. These athletes do not necessarily have to track what they eat. Implementing the tools in Chapter 7-9 will probably be sufficient for them.

IRONMAN TRAINEES

This category is for athletes that want to stay in control of their eating in spite of the increased nutritional and energy needs that go along with Ironman training. A unique mindset and high training volumes put them into a category of their own. They would like to lose a few pounds but do not want to interfere with recovery or to compromise their training. The needs of this athlete are discussed in detail in Chapter 10.

CHOOSE A TRACKING METHOD

All of the tracking methods are based upon the calorie target you calculated in Chapter 5. Each method teaches something different. Choose a method that appeals to your natural eating style (see Table 5). If you reach a plateau, move to a different method.

Counting Calories teaches you about calorie density and serving sizes. This is helpful for athletes that tend to eat high calorie foods (Hungry Meat-Eaters) and those that eat so often they don't realize how the calories add up (Grazers). This method brings the fastest results and is great for athletes that enjoy working with data.

The Visual Plate encourages you to eat from all of the food groups which helps Emotional Eaters and Grazers who tend to eat a lot of diet and low-calorie air food which lacks nutrients. This method works very well as long as you apply the 3 skills you will learn in Chapter 7 and eat Low Calorie Density food. If you fill your plate with high calorie food, you won't lose weight.

The Clean Foods approach encourages eating according to appetite rather than calorie allowance and it also encourages excellent, low-calorie nutritional choices. It is helpful for Emotional Eaters. Once you memorize the food lists, it is the easiest and most natural kind of eating.

Table 5 *Summary of Tracking Methods*

Tracking Method	Description	Easy for which eating style?	Encourages helpful change for which eating style?	Can I eat any food I want?	Do I need a calorie target?
Count Calories*	Record intake and stay within daily or weekly calorie limit	Emotional	Hungry Meat Eater Grazer	Yes, as long as you stay within the calorie limit.	Yes
Visual Plate	Eat 3 plates of food per day with set proportions of food groups	Hungry Meat Eater Ironman Trainee	Emotional Grazer	Yes, but food groups are enforced.	Yes
Clean Food	Eat certain foods until satisfied. Eat other foods in limited quantities.	Grazer Ironman Trainee Five Pounder	Emotional Hungry Meat Eater	Yes, but foods not on the list are extremely limited.	No – skip Chapter 5

*   WeightWatchers program converts calories into points values. 1 point = approx. 50 calories.

COUNTING CALORIES

RECORDING

If you can track your training data, you can track your food. In Chapter 5 you learned about the daily calorie target. Whether you went to Appendix C and calculated it or decided to use a shortcut number, you need a target for this method. Keep the total under your daily or if you prefer, weekly calorie target.

This method is only tedious (measuring and looking up calories) for a few days and less so if you prepare your Food List ahead of time (see Chapter 7) and collect all of the tools you will need before you begin. A food scale that measures both ounces and grams is essential, along with an array of measuring cups and spoons.

Your task is to list all of the foods you eat and record the number of calories. In order to calculate calories accurately, you have to measure how much you are eating. Use your measuring tools.

Don't try to keep track in your head. It is difficult and can lead to underreporting intake and ultimately, poor results. Write/record the information as you go. Don't wait until the end of the day or you will surely forget something.

If you forget to write things down, you will miss a few hundred calories here and there and your results will suffer. Poor results drain you emotionally and are frustrating. This method requires the greatest effort, but it will produce the fastest and most predictable results.

If you are already using an online training log, it may have nutrition tracking options. See *TrainingPeaks.com*, *BeginnerTriathlete.com* and *Active.com*. Other websites offer food logs with calorie count libraries. Try *Fitday.com*, *TheDailyPlate.com*, and *my-calorie-counter.com*.

The amount of time you spend weighing, measuring and tracking work will drop off quickly in about a week as you learn. You should continue to log your food intake as long as you want to lose weight. Your food logs will become valuable later, when you have reached your goal and the scale starts to creep up again (and it will). You can then use your old food logs to see precisely what you need to eat to lose weight again. Just eat the same things in the same amounts and you can shortcut the counting process.

If you don't want to go it alone, try a commercial weight loss plan that provides counseling and group support. Stay away from programs that require food purchases. There is nothing stopping you from using a commercial plan along with the tools in this book.

Sound nutrition absolutely impacts race performance. Ideally, an athlete will choose foods that give her the highest nutritional value in every calorie consumed. Table 6 sets forth nutrition recommendations for endurance athletes. Athletes should eat plenty of fruits and vegetables because of their high fiber and nutrient value. Vegetables are carbohydrates that should be eaten freely. Potatoes are the only vegetable calories you need to count.

Table 6 *Calorie breakdown – Dietary Reference Intakes from Food and Nutrition Board*

Macronutrient	% of total calories	1400 calories	1700 calories	2000 calories	2200 calories
Carbohydrate: Fruit, vegetables, whole grains, cereals, breads, pasta, sugar, sweets	60%	840	1020	1200	1320
Protein: Lean meat, fish, poultry, nonfat dairy	10%	140	170	200	220
Fat: Oil, butter, shortening, mayonnaise-based dressing and sauces	30%	420	510	600	660

Detailed information about maximizing performance through nutrition is beyond the scope of this book. The position of the American Dietetic Association, Dietitians of Canada, and the American College of Sports Medicine on nutrition and athletic performance is set forth in its entirety in Appendix D.

VISUAL PLATE

The Visual Plate (Figure 3) is adapted from the American Diabetes Association Plate Method. Instead of counting calories, fill the plate with the right portions of food. The foods that are included in each category and the calorie-specific amounts are listed in Table 7.

The 3 skills you will learn in Chapter 7 will help you manage high-calorie foods so you can continue to enjoy them in moderation.

This method works very well for athletes that like to sit down and have formal meals, or those that would prefer to tally food servings than to count calories. All of your food is divided equally into 3 plates per day. Eat it in 3 meals or eat throughout the day, just keep track of what you are eating. The worksheet in Figure 4 makes it easy to keep track.

Figure 3 *Visual Plate*

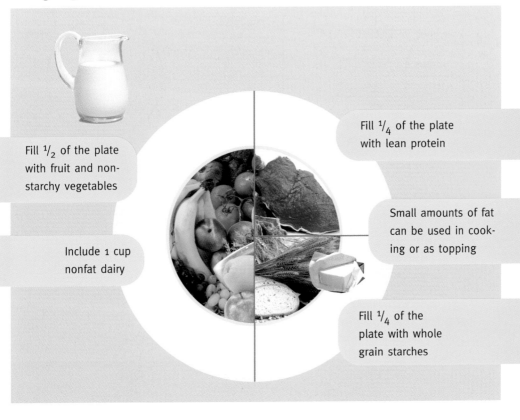

Fill ¹/₂ of the plate with fruit and non-starchy vegetables

Include 1 cup nonfat dairy

Fill ¹/₄ of the plate with lean protein

Small amounts of fat can be used in cooking or as topping

Fill ¹/₄ of the plate with whole grain starches

Figure 4 *Tracking Worksheet*

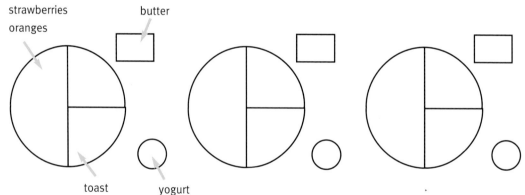

strawberries
oranges

butter

toast

yogurt

You get 3 plates per day. One quarter of each plate is for protein, one quarter is for starches and one half of each plate is for fruits and vegetables.
Dairy and fat are included in this example which works for up to 1800 calories. Higher calorie targets allow additional servings of fat.

As you eat throughout the day, mark the plates as indicated. Use the Serving Guidelines in Table 7 to estimate the amount of food in each quarter.

Table 7 *Serving Guidelines for Visual Plate (have 3/day) – My Pyramid USDA guidelines*

Type of Food / Daily calorie target	1,400	1,600	1,800	2,000	2,200	2,400	2,600
Protein: *lean meat, fish, poultry, beans, legumes, eggs, protein powder or bar*	¹/₂ deck of cards or 1.3 oz	¹/₂ deck of cards or 1.6 oz	³/₄ deck of cards or 1.7 oz	³/₄ deck of cards or 1.8 oz	2 decks of cards or 2 oz	2 ¹/₄ decks of cards or 2.2 oz	2 ¹/₂ decks of cards or 2.2 oz
Vegetables & Fruits: *unlimited amounts. count potatoes and bananas as starch, ¹/₄ avocado per day*	unlimited but at least ¹/₄ plate						
Starch: *breads, cereals, pasta, grains, starchy vegetables, sugars, 1 small dessert is entire starch and fat allotment for the meal. Carbohydrate replacement/energy bars or drinks*	1 slice or ¹/₂ cup	1 ¹/₂ slice or ³/₄ cup	2 slices or 1 cup	2 ¹/₄ slices or 1 ¹/₄ cup	2 ¹/₂ slices or 1 ¹/₂ cup	2 ³/₄ slices or 1 ³/₄ cup	3 slices or 2 cups
Fat & Oils: *nut butter, butter, cooking oil, mayonnaise, cream sauces, salad dressing nuts, cheese*	1 tsp	1 tsp	1 tsp	2 tsp	2 tsp	2 tsp	2 tsp
Nonfat Dairy: *milk, yogurt, cottage*	1 cup	1 cup	1 cup	1 cup	1 cup	1 cup	1 cup

CLEAN FOOD

If food volume is more important to you than variety, this approach is for you. If you eat only from the Clean Foods list, you don't have to count *anything*. Eat until you are satisfied but not beyond. Other foods are allowed in very limited amounts and must be counted.

There are 3 categories of food: Clean foods, Limited foods and Plus foods. The food list is in Table 8.

- **Clean Foods:** These are the foods you can eat until you are satisfied. They are very low fat, and are vitamin and fiber rich. They are not the kind of foods one is tempted to over-consume. This approach is based loosely on the WeightWatchers® Core program, promoted several years ago.

    If you eat too much, your weight loss will suffer, so don't go overboard.

- **Limited Foods:** These are foods you should limit to 2-3 servings per day. Larger athletes can have 3 servings, smaller athletes should have only 2. Nonfat dairy and starchy, high fiber carbohydrates are in this category.

- **Plus Foods:** Plus foods are anything and everything else. Limit these to 100 calories per day or 700 per week.

Table 8 *Clean Food List*

Clean foods:
- All fruits and vegetables except potatoes and bananas. $^1/_2$ avocado/day.
- Clear broths and broth based soups without pasta or rice.
- Diet soda, coffee, unsweetened tea, drinks with less than 10 calories per cup.
- Beans & legumes; fresh, frozen or canned without fat.
- Lean, skinless meat; poultry, fish, shellfish, beef, pork, game. Fresh, frozen or canned and water-packed. Ground meats with 10% fat or less. Low-fat or fat-free hot dogs, fat-free breaded frozen chicken products.
- Vinegars, salsa, condiments, sugar and fat-free dressings and sauces.
- Air popped corn
- Sugar-free Jell-O

Limited Foods: *2-3 servings/day. Eat 3/day if your calorie target exceeds 2000 calories/day*

- Nonfat dairy including milk, cottage cheese, yogurt, sugar-free pudding (1 cup serving)
- Whole Grains including breads, whole grain pasta, brown rice, unsweetened cereals exceeding 5 g fiber per serving. (3 oz serving)

Plus:
- 100 daily calories of anything else you want that is not a clean food.

7 Three Skills

· ·

> People say to me all the time, "Whoa! You do triathlons?
> You must be able to eat whatever you want!"
> To which I reply: "You have no idea how much I want."
>
> – Jayne Williams, Slow Fat Triathlete

Now that you have chosen a tracking method, what are you supposed to eat? People tend to eat a consistent amount of food from day to day. The amount is based on food *weight*, not calories [53]. An effective eating plan will cut calories *without* reducing the amount (weight) of food you can eat [54]. This is done by eating less high calorie density (HCD) food and more low calorie density (LCD) food. "Calorie density" describes the number of calories per mouthful.

Weight management becomes relatively easy once you learn how to combine HCD and LCD foods so that you can eat what you enjoy and eat enough to satisfy your appetite. You can apply these skills to any food, but HCD foods are the most important ones to manage:

1. Limit
2. Substitute
3. Modify

These 3 skills will help with all of the tracking methods described in Chapter 6. Before you can use them, you have to know which foods are HCD and which ones aren't. The best way to start is to learn about the foods you typically eat.

MAKE A FOOD LIST

The food list (Table 9) will help you identify which foods are high in calorie density and which ones are low. Once you have done this, you can use the 3 skills to manage those foods.

There are many online calculators/food lists to ease the process of looking up calorie and fat counts for the foods you have listed. These include: *www.nutritiondata.com*, *www.thedailyplate.com*, *www.freedieting.com* and *www.caloriecontrol.org*. Creating an online food log is helpful, but you will also need a paper copy to keep in your kitchen, car and office. You will need access to the information whenever a food issue arises.

Once you have completed the worksheet, you can identify the High Calorie Density foods (calorie bombs), and the LCD foods (calorie bargains).

How to complete the Food List:
- List all of the foods in each category that you typically eat, then record the calories and fat grams per serving.
- Combination foods like casseroles are difficult. The best way is to look up each ingredient separately, but don't count the vegetables or spices. The only vegetable worth counting is potatoes. Count all the other ingredients.
- Assume that fat based sauces/dressings/ toppings (that contain cream, cream soups, butter, oil) have 120 calories per tablespoon.

Table 9 *Food List*

Food Type	Foods I eat in this category, calories & fat per serving
Breads, bakery items, pastries	
Pasta, rice, grains, warm and cold cereals	
Fruits, juices, dried and frozen	
Butter, oil, shortening, sauces, toppings, dips	
Fast food	
Take-out food	
Meat, fish, poultry, sausage, hot dogs, deli/processed	
Dairy-cheeses, yogurt, milk, eggs	
Vegetables canned fresh frozen	
Soups	
Casseroles, stews, ethnic cuisine, combination foods	
Desserts, pastries, candy, chocolates, pie, cake, ice cream	

Food Type	Foods I eat in this category, calories & fat per serving
Nuts, nut spreads	
Drinks, sodas, juices	
Snack foods	
Beans, lentils, soy products	
Other	
Training fuels-carbo-hydrate/electrolyte replacements, gels, bars, recovery shakes	

Once you have completed your list, you should identify which foods are High Calorie Density. HCD foods are those that:

1. Exceed 10 grams of fat per serving, and/or
2. Exceed 300 calories per serving.

The HCD foods are the ones you will limit, substitute or modify as explained below. That does not mean you have to stop eating them, only that you must manage them to reduce their calorie impact. The skills described in the next section will help you do that.

THE 3 SKILLS

The 3 skills will help you mange the HCD foods on your food list, and any others you encounter.

The skills can be applied however you wish. There is no single correct way to manage any particular food. You can limit, substitute or modify any food. When you want to eat a HCD food, ask yourself:

1. Do I really want to eat it? (limit)
2. If yes, is it a food I can substitute with a LCD alternative? (substitute)
3. If not, can I combine with other LCD foods to reduce the calorie density? (modify)

Some HCD foods will be easy for you to avoid or limit, while others are so central to your diet that you will feel deprived if you don't have them often. Some foods are easy to modify by combining them with LCD foods to dilute their calorie density. Still other foods are convenient and satisfactory to substitute. You decide which action to take.

HOW TO APPLY THE 3 SKILLS

Now that you have identified the HCD foods in your diet, Table 10 has suggestions for applying the 3 skills to those foods.

Table 10 *What to do with common HCD Foods*

Common HCD Foods	Ways to limit, substitute or modify
Alcohol	Avoid/ limit to once a week. Modify by diluting with diet soda, sugar free mixer, or fruit juice. White wine and light beer are less calorie-dense.
Baked sweets (commercially made)	Substitute with homemade and modify using 50% less oil/shortening. If too dry, use some nonfat milk/ applesauce to supplement oil. Diet Soda can be used as sole wet ingredient in most cake mixes.
Butter, mayonnaise, salad dressings	Small amounts. Substitute/ modify with mustard, salsa, fruit juice, low fat versions, nonfat dairy balsamic and other flavored vinegars.
Canned Frosting	Avoid as much as possible. These products are nearly 100% fat. Substitute with homemade or with flavored syrups and lite whipped topping.
Cheese based foods-pizza, lasagna, enchiladas, macaroni & cheese, cheese/ garlic bread, cheese sauce	Remove most cheese/serve on a bed of LCD bulk like shredded lettuce, cabbage, salad greens, vegetables.
Carbohydrate and protein bars powders and drinks	Substitute with real food.
Donuts and pastries	Avoid/limit. Modify by sprinkling small pieces on lite whipped topping and fruit.
Dried fruit	Fresh fruits provide more bulk and satiety.
Fast food	Choose grilled chicken w/out cheese. No mayonnaise-based sauces (See Chapter 8).

Fried foods-meats, potatoes, vegetables	Grilled, roasted, baked, broiled, boiled, steamed, "lightly sautéed".
Full fat dairy products, heavy cream, milk, cottage cheese, yogurt, ice cream	Substitute with nonfat versions, (sorbet, sherbert) or "slow churned" ice cream.
Nuts, nut butters	Use sparingly. Substitute with melted nonfat cottage cheese
Pork or beef ribs, bacon, processed meats, hot dogs, sausage. Fatty cuts of beef-rib eye, prime rib, filet mignon, ground beef exceeding 10% fat	Remove visible fat. Limit amount. Modify by using meat as a condiment with compatible vegetables. Substitute with: leaner cuts like flank steak, sirloin and tri-tip, low fat deli meats, fat-free hot dogs, Canadian bacon, turkey sausage and bacon.
Soda, sweetened beverages, fruit juices	Substitute with water or diet soda if you must.
Visible fat/skin on any cut of meat	Avoid. Remove skin (after cooking), drain fat before making sauces.

HOW TO LIMIT HCD FOOD

Limiting a food does not mean you have to eliminate it. It means eat as little of it as possible. Here are some ways to do that:

1. Don't keep the food in the house. If you must, go out and have it in a restaurant. Don't keep the leftovers.

2. If it ends up in your house, eat a single serving then immediately discard the leftovers.

3. Eat it as infrequently as possible.

4. Include it in your post-workout meal following your longest training session. See Chapter 9.

THE 10 GRAM RULE

There is still some controversy over optimum daily fat intake, especially for athletes. But there is no reason to eat foods that are brimming with added fat. Read labels and avoid anything that has more than 10 grams of fat per serving. That said, you can still eat these foods but in very limited quantities and on rare occasions. Since it is a HCD food, you will only be able to "afford" a bite or two, but it may be worth it. It is your call.

High Calorie Density starches and desserts:
A normal size chocolate chip cookie usually does not exceed 10 grams of fat, but a pancake-sized one does. Low-fat and even some regular ice creams are within this limit. "slow-churned" ice cream has less calorie density because it has extra air it, making it literally, lighter by weight without adding artificial fats or sweeteners. Nonfat frozen yogurt is a good substitute too.

If you decide you want ice cream or anything else that is calorie dense, read the labels until you find one that is acceptable from a fat standpoint. There are large brand to brand variations in the fat content of ice creams, frozen confections, candy bars (those with nuts and nut based fillings are higher), baking mixes for cakes and cookies, pie crusts, and even breads. If you can't stay within the 10 gram rule, buy the lowest fat alternative available.

High Calorie Density fats:

The 10 gram rule applies to more than desserts. What about fatty meat and cheese? Rather than eliminate these foods, eat them in small amounts but get the most satisfaction from them. For example, a stew made with prime rib is a good way to add volume, but saturating the meat in a flavored sauce doesn't allow the taste of the beef to come through. If you are going to have prime rib or sausage or pizza for that matter, eat a few bites that you will really enjoy.

Roasted chicken skin is tasty, but you can do without the fat. You can cook chicken without the skin but it will be terribly dry. Instead, cook the chicken with the skin on to get some of the taste, then remove it before eating or have a small piece of skin that you cut into tiny pieces. Have a little piece of skin with each bite of lean meat. Count the skin as a serving of fat.

Cheese is another example. Generally, flavor is enhanced in cold foods. Melted cheddar cheese does not taste as strong as room temperature cheese. If you crave cheddar cheese, have it cold and separate it from other foods. Cheese sprinkled over a salad gets lost in the other flavors so why bother? You can take this a step further and get the most flavor-intense option available. A small amount of sharp cheddar will give you more taste than mild cheddar will.

CALORIC DRINKS

Avoid liquid calories. Researchers have concluded that total calorie intake is significantly higher on days when you drink soda, alcohol, milk and juice as opposed to the days when only water is consumed [55].

It makes sense. Liquids are heavy, but since they don't stay in your stomach very long, they don't contribute to the "food weight" you are used to consuming each day. They don't keep you satisfied. Your goal is to get the maximum satisfaction out of every calorie. When possible, eat the solid form instead of the liquid. An orange instead of orange juice, cottage cheese instead of milk, etc.

Plain coffee and tea are calorie free but be careful with what is added to them. A nonfat latte is very low calorie but adding syrup and cream makes it into a calorie nightmare. Many varieties of tea are highly sweetened so be careful.

The carbohydrate drinks you wolf down during and after training are not necessary if you are focused on weight loss and training at maintenance levels. The consumption of training-related fuel is discussed in Chapter 9. Alcohol is also trouble. It influences appetite, metabolism and resolve. See Chapter 8.

HOW TO CHOOSE HCD FOOD

If you absolutely must eat a particular HCD food, pick the one that will give you the greatest satisfaction. Sometimes, the only food that will satisfy you is one particular brand. In that case, go ahead and eat it. There are times when a craving will not be satisfied any other way and you can end up eating a large quantity (and more calories) of a poor substitute and still be left unsatisfied. If you are not married to one particular brand, look for the one that is the least calorie dense. That means you can eat more of it for a given number of calories.

You will be surprised how much variation there is among brands. Compare the labels and look at the following:

1. Which has the lowest number of calories per serving?
2. Which as the least amount of fat?
3. Which has the largest serving size?

Be careful with serving sizes. A quick glance at a label can make you think a food isn't too bad. The serving size for a high calorie food is often smaller than a normal serving. Manufacturers label foods this way to mislead you into believing you are getting a lower calorie food.

SUBSTITUTIONS

Looking back at your food list, there are probably some foods that have more calories than you expected. There are 3 ways to substitute HCD foods:

1. Use the diet or low calorie version of the food.
2. Use a lower fat version of the food.
3. Use a higher fiber version of the food.

The easy way is to buy a "diet" product but sometimes the low calorie product is so tasteless it is not worth eating. Fat-free cheese is an example. If all you are looking for is texture, maybe the fat-free cheese will work, but if taste matters, you are better off eating a few shreds of real cheese.

Using vegetables as a substitute for starchy food is one of the best ways to dramatically reduce calories, increase nutrient value and to stay full longer. Below are some examples of food substitutions. Use your food list for ideas and experiment. You can also find substitutions online at *www.fitnessandfreebies.com*, *www.nhlbi.nih.gov* and *www.goodhousekeeping.com*.

When you can, substitute with a product that has more fiber, even if the calorie content is the same. Fiber is important because it does not digest so it makes food bulky without adding calories. It takes longer to digest and literally keeps your stomach full longer. Fibrous fruits and vegetables and whole grain products are examples of high fiber foods. A growing selection of starchy carbohydrates (bread, pasta, cereal) are available in whole grain versions.

Substitute vegetables for starches and meats:
- Serve spaghetti sauce over a bed of steamed vegetables instead of pasta
- Substitute a lettuce leaf for the top of a hamburger bun.
- Use vinegars and fruit juices instead of salad dressing, or use a "diet" brand.
- Substitute mustard in place of mayonnaise.
- Instead of serving a taco in a shell, make it into a taco salad.

Meat substitutions:
- Substitute beans for meat where possible.
- Serve a grilled Portobello mushroom instead of ground beef to make a

hamburger. Choose leaner meats over high fat cuts.

- Choose poultry instead of beef.
- The butcher will grind lean turkey or chicken to use instead of beef.
- Eat fish instead of red meat whenever possible.

Add moisture to HCD foods by substituting the following for gravy/butter/oil/sauce:

- Nonfat milk
- Nonfat plain yogurt instead of sour cream
- Salsa
- Flavored vinegar
- Clear broth
- Nonfat cottage cheese (adds some protein too)

How to eat pizza:

Minimize the calorie density of pizza by ordering a thin crust, topped with vegetables and no cheese. If you absolutely must have cheese, take most of it off and have a bite or two (100 calories per bite). Use Canadian bacon instead of sausage or pepperoni.

AIR FOOD

Fruits and vegetables are great LCD choices from a nutrition standpoint, but they do not satisfy the desire for salty crunchiness. Air food is high volume, LCD food that keeps your mouth busy. Unlike "diet" foods, air foods are naturally this way. Examples include: rice cakes, air-popped corn, unsweetened puffed rice and puffed wheat cereals. When the munchies hit, air food is a good place to start.

BE CAUTIOUS WITH "DIET" FOODS

Watch out for foods that say "diet," "reduced fat," "no sugar added" or "sugar-free" on the label. These foods are usually Low Calorie Density but they always have some combination of added artificial fats (like Olestra) and artificial sweeteners (NutraSweet, Sorbitol and Saccharin). Reduced fat foods often have extra sugar in them so the calories can still be high.

1. They don't taste very good. You are better off eating a small amount of the real food than wasting your time on these fakes. They add calories but little else. If you find some foods in this category that are good, keep them on hand but you still need to count the calories.

2. There is evidence that eating artificially sweetened foods increases or at least reinforces your desire for sweet foods [56]. This is particularly true with diet soda.

3. The artificial fats and sweeteners tend to bring on at the very least, mild gas, and at worst, explosive diarrhea. Having one or two sugar free candies in the morning can wreak havoc on an afternoon run. Products like Beano® and simethicone help with the gas, but you may still feel bloated. If you must eat gas-producing stuff, do so after you are done with your training for the day.

NONFAT IS GOOD

Don't confuse diet foods with "nonfat" or "fat free," "lean" or "extra lean" foods. These foods generally do not have anything added to them to substitute for the fat. These more naturally nonfat foods are good LCD choices that will not cause the problems associated with "diet" foods.

"VEGETARIAN" IS NOT ALWAYS BETTER

Vegetarian foods do not have any animal-derived additives. If you are worried about fat, the word "vegetarian" only means that the fat that is in the product is from plants rather than animals. Vegetable based fat is just as HCD as animal fat.

MODIFICATIONS

MODIFY NORMAL FOOD

Eating food that is different from what the rest of the family is eating is costly, stressful and banishes you to a sort of social isolation. Eating normal food is an important skill that will allow you to fit in no matter where you are. But how do you minimize the calories? You modify the food so it is not so calorie dense. There are several ways to do this and creativity can pay off. It will seem strange at first but it gets easier and more interesting as time goes on. Here are some ways to modify normal food.

Remove HCD components:
- Remove skin and visible fats from meat.
- Remove cheese.

Combine small portions of HCD food with larger volumes of LCD food.
Here are some ways to add bulk to small portions of HCD main dish foods:
- Serve them in/on vegetables like shredded lettuce, shredded cabbage, bagged salad, spaghetti squash, stewed tomatoes, mushrooms, celery.
- Make them into combination dishes like vegetable based chili, casseroles, stews and soups.
- Serve a tiny portion of HCD dessert with sugar free angel food cake, fresh berries, fat free frozen yogurt or lite whipped topping.
- Dilute the calorie impact of sauces, toppings and dressings by using $1/_3$ the amount of high fat oil/butter/mayonnaise/cream and mixing in some nonfat dairy like milk, yogurt, sour cream or dairy. You have to experiment to find the proportions that preserve most of the taste.

8 Tools for Success

"We never repent of having eaten too little."

– Thomas Jefferson

TOOLS

This chapter provides a mountain of tools and instructions for using them. The tools will help you maintain focus and to apply the 3 skills when circumstances threaten to derail you. The tools are listed in Table 11 at the end of the chapter.

The main difficulty with calorie restriction is getting too hungry. The 3 skills from Chapter 7 will help tremendously, but the first few days are always a challenge. Hunger tools will help you manage your appetite.

Another problem with restricting calories is eating in social situations. Going to parties and family get-togethers is only part of it. We deal with family everyday and with our co-workers all week. Lack of control over food offerings and social expectations can make it a chore to stay on task. Social Tools will keep you on track when you are with others.

Dining out is a challenge whether it is take-out, fast food, or a traditional restaurant. It is important to know what to order to keep your intake in line with your goals. Dining out tools will help you know what to eat when you aren't at home.

The first section is about the important things you should do every day to stay with your program.

DAILY PRACTICES
(MAKING WEIGHT CONTROL AN EVERYDAY REALITY)

ACCOUNTABILITY

In this context, accountability is "officially" weighing in on a weekly basis and reporting the result to someone (or to yourself). Doing so forces you to accept the choices you made that week and to move forward to the next one with a clean slate.

Accountability is also encouraged in commercial weight management programs that include regular cell phone, text message or email contact with a counselor. These programs that incorporate weight related support along with regular contact have been quite effective [57, 58].

Jesse lost 36 pounds in 15 weeks and now has 11% body fat. He says "This (sic) has been the most helpful; my wife and my neighbor/best friend participated in a program together and all kept each other accountable with the workouts and the diets."

ACKNOWLEDGE SUCCESS

Every bit of progress should be acknowledged. Define progress as behavior that moves you toward controlling your weight. It can be making a good choice, throwing away a half-eaten cake that has been tempting you, or foregoing your usual cola for water. You need not throw a party, but mentally, add another victory to your list and be strengthened by it.

MODIFY BOTHERSOME HABITS

Sometimes eating is a way of relaxing at the end of the day. There is nothing wrong with that as long as you can still find a way to lose weight. Habits do not have to be broken if they serve you well. Snacking after dinner is a prime example. So many people feel like failures at weight control because they like to snack at night and that is a shame. As long as you track what you eat and you can still lose weight, there is nothing wrong with eating at night. Focus on the total amount of food you eat – that is what matters for weight management.

If you have a habit that you want to change, break the pattern by doing something different. Change something about the activity to interrupt the usual flow. You could try watching TV in a different room upstairs, away from the kitchen. If you want to really shake things up, put on a pair of high heels before you start to snack (women only – I think). Bill O'Hanlon's book, *Do One Thing Different* (Morrow, 1999) is loaded with interesting ways to change habits.

PAY ATTENTION TO HUNGER

Some people eat only when they are hungry. Most eat for hunger and a multitude of other reasons. Pay attention to your hunger and strive to eat according to those signals rather than out of emotion or habit. You will be better off in the long run.

RECORD YOUR WEIGHT DAILY

There is evidence that daily weighing helps you keep weight off [59]. Staying off the scale is in vogue, but it is important for serious, committed weight controllers. Daily weighing has many advantages:

- The only way to become familiar with how much your weight fluctuates from day to day is to weigh yourself daily. It demonstrates that the variability in your weight is based on what you eat, how you train, your monthly cycle and your training load.

- Knowing the typical range of your weight fluctuations will help you distinguish a true weight gain from a temporary one. When you have achieved your lifelong weight, it is important to take action quickly when you put on a few pounds. Knowing your normal weight patterns will help you to recognize when you must act. Weighing daily will let you nip a weight gain in the bud so you can act on it when it is still tiny. It is also harder to deny a weight gain when it is staring you in the face day after day. Get into the habit now. It will help you in the future.

- You may see temporary weight gains following long training rides when you have consumed electrolytes and carbohydrates which tend to make you retain water. You may also see an increase after rigorous strength training sessions when you are sore. Some of this soreness is an inflammatory process in the muscles as they recover. These changes in the scale are not fat increases so they should not alarm you.

- Weighing often (and recording your weight) will eventually dampen the emotional impact of an unexpected gain or loss. This is important because some people will see an unexpected weight loss as a cause for celebration and an invitation to slacken their food control for a few days. This can cause a weight gain. It is also important to overcome your emotional attachment to the scale. It is a tool that displays a number. How you manage the information is within your control. Taking control of your food includes taking control of your scale too.

- Salty foods like soy sauce can raise your weight several pounds overnight. Consider what you have been eating. Remember that water comes and goes in a matter of hours. To gain a pound of fat requires overeating 3,500 calories. Do you *really* believe that your weight is up 4 pounds from yesterday because of the 700 calorie piece of cake you ate yesterday? Give your weight a few days to return to normal. Don't be a weight alarmist.

- The other scenario is getting overly discouraged by unexpected weight gain, and turning to food for comfort. Being used to weight fluctuations will keep you away from food as a form of celebration or stress relief.

- Knowing your weight keeps you honest. Even if you do not eat excess calories and gain weight, what you put into your body has an immediate impact on the scale. Sometimes it is helpful to weigh more than once a day. Before and after workouts will tell you about your sweat rate. If you have trouble remembering to do this, keep a scale in the garage next to your bike so you are reminded to record your weight before and after you ride.

- If you are trying to control after dinner eating, weighing several times a day may help. A 2004 study had people record their weight *four times* a day. The people that were significantly heavier before bedtime were more likely to gain weight than the ones whose weights remained stable throughout the day [61].

RENEW MOTIVATION

Renew your motivation everyday. Imagine your life at your new weight. See yourself making the right decisions to get you there. Go ahead and plan on success. Get the new racing outfit that you will fit into. Behave as if achieving your goal is a foregone conclusion. Make it who you are. See Chapter 12 for more on motivation.

THROW IT OUT

Believe it or not, throwing food out is an important and for some, a difficult skill. Our reluctance to waste food comes mostly from family history and cultural norms. In some people the little voice inside scolds them about wasting food. It is up to you how to argue with that voice but on a practical level, you don't want to do anything that offends someone you care about. Don't launch your aunt's cheesecake into the bin in front of her face. Wait until she is gone. Be polite. Be discrete but get rid of it before it becomes a temptation.

When you are alone and you start to hear a food calling to you, take control. Throw it away. Sometimes the trash can is not enough, so put it down the sink.

The choice is pretty clear. Either you remove the food from your environment or you will eventually give in and wear it on your thighs or your gut. You can shortcut the process by attaching the offending food to your skin directly with some duct tape.

Getting rid of junky food has another perk; it makes you feel *powerful*.
Don't worry about the financial impact. Eating food you don't want to eat, putting on weight and suffering the emotional pain of a weight problem is more costly than the food you toss out.

TIME BETWEEN MEALS

Spacing meals and snacks 2-3 hours apart gives you a chance to get hungry and gives your body a break from processing food all the time. Modify the munching habit by forcing food breaks. Start with one break per day and expand up to 3, but don't make the breaks longer than 3 hours.

TRACK WHAT YOU EAT

It doesn't matter which method you use, you still should record what and how much you eat. If you don't at least record *what* you eat you will have difficulty figuring out where you are going wrong if you aren't losing weight.

Recording your food intake requires some organization. At home, have a pad in the kitchen and write things down immediately. Use your computer, email, cell phone, PDA or a small notebook to keep track. You can also add a food list to your training log. The more detailed your list, the more helpful it will be.

TRAIN TO MAINTAIN

Keep training, but focus your efforts on weight loss rather than performance gains. It is difficult to lose weight and keep your muscles bursting with glycogen at the same time.

Shoot for about 6-8 training hours per week. Successful weight losers get that much physical activity even if they are not "triathletes" [61]. This level of activity should be normal for you for the rest of your life. Strength training should also be part of your main-tenance routine (see Chapter 9).

© jimcox40/fotolia.com

SOCIAL TOOLS

(STAY ON TRACK WHEN YOU ARE WITH OTHERS)

ATTITUDE

The most powerful tool you have in social situations is your attitude. If you exude certainty, others will accept it. If you express doubt, others will exploit it. Comments from people you care about do have an impact, even though your are a tough triathlete. If your attitude is based on the belief that you will not fail, comments will not weaken your resolve. If you feel vulnerable to social pressure, don't make a pronouncement about your weight loss plan, just take the steps and lose the weight.

PERSONAL SUPPORT

Losing weight will be easier if the immediate family supports your effort. The main objection family members have to your weight loss plan is the change in meals and foods available to *them*. Eating better should not cause a ruckus in the household. You don't have to go crazy and strip the house of foods the rest of your family enjoys, be smart and limit the foods that tempt *you*. Use the skills from Chapter 7 and keep eating normal food. After a few days the family will get on board.

When it comes to co-workers and extended family, it is often best to keep your efforts to yourself and let them *see* the results over time. Making a big deal over you new "food plan" will put the focus and pressure on you. They won't know what food to offer you. Announcing your intentions also creates pressure in your own psyche. It is really no one's business what you eat and the less you call attention to it, to more natural it will be for you. Your new way of eating is not temporary, it is a new reality that will stay with you the rest of your life.

Another avenue of support is what you read. There are plenty of inspiring and lighthearted books about weight loss that will help you feel less alone in your quest. See *Heft of Wheels* by Mike Magnuson (Harmony, 2004), Judy Gruen's *Till We Eat Again: Confessions of a Diet Dropout* (Champion, 2002) and *Slow Fat Triathlete: Live Your Athletic Dreams in the Body You Have Now* by Jayne Williams (Da Cappo, 2004)

SAY "NO THANKS"

Saying no to food in social settings can be a dicey proposition, depending upon who is offering the food and how they expect you to react. There is no reason that an adult should have to eat, even "just a bite" of something they don't want. Saying, "no thank you" is a polite response and it should end the matter but often it doesn't work that way.

Relinquishing control of what you eat to anyone else is a bad idea. What do you think it means to be in control of your food? It means that you call the shots, every day, all day.

The person offering you the food does not realize that even "one bite" of something has a psychological and chemical consequence. A taste of sugar can set in motion a craving for the stuff that you will have to battle the rest of the day... all because of one little bite.

You should become familiar with particular foods that can trigger your appetite. For some, it is salty crunchy chips; for others, sweets, and still others are triggered by starches. Although calorically speaking, you need not eliminate any particular food to lose weight, you should stay away from foods that set into motion an intense desire for more.

Family politics are up to you to manage. If food is offered and you can't refuse without someone causing a scene, take it, but don't eat it. When you can, throw it in the trash, the yard, or just leave it with the dirty dishes.

A single bite of something can trigger a craving, it can provide 100 or more unwanted calories and worst of all, it can make you feel that *someone else* is in control of your eating instead of you.

SOCIAL OCCASIONS, CELEBRATIONS AND HOLIDAYS

With planning you can get through a holiday party unscathed. Eating something healthy before you go to an event will take the edge off your hunger. Bringing an appetizer and some fruit that you can eat freely is a thoughtful contribution to the festivities and gives you something to munch on. Here are some other ideas:

- If you fear you will be faced with high-fat food choices for more than a few hours, it may be worthwhile to bring a cooler and some of your own food. Don't make an announcement about it. Keep it discrete. At a lively party, most people will not notice what you are eating or where you got it.
- Offer to go to the grocery store for a quick reprieve from the crowd and for a chance to buy some food that you can eat.
- Bring a 6-pack of diet soda to share.
- In a pinch, sneak a Power Bar or Ensure to tide you over until mealtime.

STOP SAMPLING

When you go to the local warehouse store, the lunchtime sample tables are everywhere and for many the samples accumulate into a free meal. Perhaps they are free in terms of money but they are certainly not free in terms of calories. Those little nibbles add up quickly. Don't even start. Just walk away. You can do it.

Another source of sampling temptation is with your kids. Stop sampling your kid's French fries. Stop taking a spoonful of their ice cream or a bite of birthday cake. See Say "No Thanks" above.

WEIGHT-RELATED SUPPORT

Weight loss programs that incorporate behavioral treatment, diet change, and encouragement of physical activity improve your psychological state and your mood [62]. Support can be one on one, or in groups.

Men aren't usually comfortable at traditional weight support meetings, but there are alternatives. With the internet and cell phones, online or phone supported weight loss programs are widely available. WeightWatchers® has group support and online support and online program especially for men.

The idea of traditional group support may be unappealing because as an athlete, you think you will not have much in common with the mostly older women you see at a typical WeightWatchers® meeting. This perception is correct to some degree, but on the other hand, food issues are food issues, no matter who has them. You may be surprised how much you have in common with those ladies when it comes to food. Your athleticism obviously puts you way ahead of the game when it comes to exercise, but just imagine how helpful your comments will be. Give it a try and you will be pleasantly surprised how much positive information is available at group support meetings.

HUNGER TOOLS
(MANAGE YOUR APPETITE)

AVOID ALCOHOL

There is controversy about some aspects of how alcohol consumption influences health. From a weight management standpoint, alcohol is trouble.

1. Alcohol is more calorically dense than carbohydrate or protein. It is an HCD food.
2. It has virtually no nutritional value.
3. It suppresses the number of fat calories your body burns for energy, replacing fat as a source of fuel [63, 64].
4. It stimulates hunger [65].
5. It impairs judgment, making it harder to stick to your food program.
6. It reduces testosterone levels especially after exercise [66] which may explain why people who drink a lot of alcohol carry less muscle [67].

Strategies for reducing alcohol intake include:
• Limit intake to one day per week.
• Limit the amount to one or two glasses.
• Drink a large glass of water before an alcoholic drink.
• Keep water next to you and drink it between sips of alcohol.
• Reduce calorie density by mixing the alcohol with a diet soda. Add lemon-lime soda to white wine to make a "spritzer".

CONTROL DAILY TREATS

Part of managing your appetite is dealing with cravings. If there is an HCD food that you crave every day, it may be better to have a little than to feel deprived all the time.

Having a small piece of chocolate every day is perfectly fine as long as you have control over it. If it makes you feel good, allow yourself a small amount (about 100 calories worth) of your favorite thing every day. Just make sure you account for it and if it triggers you, or if you start eating more than your daily allotment, get rid of it immediately. Control, not deprivation, is the key.

Having daily access to your favorites makes them seem less indulgent. By having them available their power over you is diminished. It is just food.

CONTROL FOOD VARIETY

Novel foods stimulate the reward pathways in the brain that tell you to eat, even if you are not hungry. In other words, you eat more when there are lots of yummy choices. This is one reason people eat more food at a restaurant buffet than when they are at home [68].

With this in mind, if you want to eat more of a certain kind of food, you should have a large variety of it around. Most athletes will benefit from eating more vegetables, fruit and lean protein (LCD foods). These foods are the cornerstone of good nutrition, superior performance, and controlling hunger. Since you will benefit from eating more Low Calorie Density foods, you should have a variety of them available [69].

Likewise, you want to eat less High Calorie Density food; you shouldn't tempt yourself, so it is helpful to keep fewer of these foods around. Less variety means less temptation. People who successfully maintain weight loss eat a small variety of foods, especially the HCD kind [70].

EAT PROTEIN

Eating protein will control feelings of hunger so include some in every meal [71, 72]. A spoonful of nonfat cottage cheese as a supplement for your snack or meal provides a nice boost. It has only 40 calories, no fat and 7 grams (28 calories) of protein.

If protein is not consumed within 24-48 hours after a training session, changes (growth, repair) in muscle will not occur.

Protein has positive effects for men and women. In women, consuming a diet with 30% of the calories from protein increases satiety [71]. Men get even more benefit; such a diet improves fat oxidation, keeps energy levels high and builds muscle. All of these changes are related to weight loss [72].

HAVE ACCESS TO SAFE SNACKS

Your home should be a safe and restful place. When you get hungry, you should be able to find healthy LCD foods to munch on. All it takes is planning. By keeping tempting, poor quality foods out of your house, you can keep that little junk food voice from calling your name. Instead, stock up on safe foods like fruits, vegetables, and "air foods" like air popped corn.

You will also get hungry at work or in your car so make those areas safe as well. Keep a cooler in your car stocked with bulky, LCD food. If you can remember to keep an ice block in your cooler you will have even more options. Bringing your own lunch is the best way to control what you eat.

Having food in your car will also keep you from seeking fast food out of hunger. A 350 calorie can of protein drink is no calorie bargain, but it is much better than succumbing to a fast food binge because you are starving. Protein shakes do not need refrigeration so you can keep them in your car for emergencies without a cooler.

Along the same lines, don't bring HCD junk foods into your house or your workplace. Do not fall victim to the excuse of buying junk "for the kids" or "for my husband" or for "the guys at work." You are not fooling anyone but yourself. Create an environment that *guarantees* success.

LEFTOVERS FOR LATER

Make extra servings of healthy delicious dishes and freeze the leftovers in single serving containers. Reheating in the microwave takes only a few minutes and having a tasty and nutritious choice available will make it easier to resist other convenient, but poor quality foods.

MAKE RECIPES FOR SUCCESS

You will be hungry in the first few days of your weight loss program. A cup of warm soup is a quick and satisfying snack. Here are 2 recipes for soup that are simple to make and they taste good. You can eat the vegetable soup in unlimited portions.

Don't limit yourself to these. LCD recipes can be found at: *www.eatingwell.com*, *www.Allrecipies.com*, *www.foodnetwork.com* and countless other websites.

Mexican Can Soup

Don't drain the cans. This is a Clean Food that you do not have to count if you are using that approach.

- 12 oz can stewed tomatoes in chunks
- 12 oz can pinto beans
- 12 oz can corn
- $1/2$ envelope/ 2 Tbs. taco seasoning
- 12 oz can black beans
- 12 oz can red beans
- 1 medium onion sliced thin
- $1/2$ envelope of dry ranch dressing mix

Directions: Brown the onion in a tiny amount of olive oil and water until it is tender. Pour the entire can ingredients, juice and all, into the pot along with the spices. Simmer for 10 min.

- Serve as taco or burrito filling.
- Serve over shredded lettuce or cabbage with fat free sour cream and a few crumbled tortilla chips.

Vegetable Soup

- $2/3$ cup sliced carrots
- $1/2$ cup diced onions
- $1/2$ cup green beans
- 1 $1/2$ cups diced green cabbage
- $1/2$ teaspoon dried basil
- $1/4$ teaspoon salt
- 2 minced garlic cloves
- 3 cups fat-free broth (beef, chicken or vegetable)
- 1 tablespoon tomato paste
- $1/4$ teaspoon dried oregano
- $1/2$ cup diced zucchini

Directions: Brown onions in small amount of olive oil and water. Add broth and all other ingredients. Salt & pepper to taste. Simmer and enjoy.

TOOLS FOR DINING OUT
(WHAT TO EAT NO MATTER WHERE YOU GO)

HOW TO EAT AT A RESTAURANT

Avoid Fat:
Limit oil, butter, dressings, sauces, cheese. You don't have to count every fat gram, just eat as little as you can.

Go Green:
Fill at least half of your plate with steamed green vegetables. Potatoes and corn should be considered "starches" and eaten in smaller amounts.

Hand & Fist rule:
If you absolutely must order a fatty cut of meat or a calorie calamity like lasagna, eat a serving no larger than the palm of your hand (if it is flat) or your fist (if it is not).

HOW TO EAT FAST FOOD

If you plan right, you will always have access to healthy delicious food at home, at work and even in your car and you will never have to go to a fast food restaurant. The only thing worse than a fast food restaurant is a convenience store attached to a gas station. There is little there that is worth eating.

Be prepared with a list of acceptable foods you can eat at each fast-food outlet you are likely to come across and keep it in your car/in your cell phone at all times. Most fast food restaurants have nutrition information online.

If you must eat fast food:
- Choose grilled chicken over beef.
- Avoid cheese, nut toppings, bacon, mayonnaise, sauces, butter, salad dressings (other than low-fat dressing which should be used sparingly) and anything fried.
- Choose fresh fruit side dishes when that is an option.
- Drink water instead of soda, diet soda if you must.
- Skip the fries. They are about 10 calories each.
- Sandwich shops are much better than hamburger places. Go for the low fat version, no oil, cheese or mayo. Stick with turkey or skinless chicken.

Table 11 *Summary of tools for success*

Tools	
Daily Practices	Accountability
	Acknowledge success
	Modify habits
	Pay attention to hunger
	Record weight
	Renew motivation
	Throw it out
	Time between meals
	Track what you eat
	Train to maintain
Social Tools	Attitude
	Personal support
	Say "No thanks"
	Social occasions
	Stop sampling
	Weight-related support
Hunger Tools	Avoid alcohol
	Control daily treats
	Control food variety
	Eat protein
	Have access to safe snacks
	Leftovers for later
	Make recipes
Tools for dining out	Avoid fat
	Go green
	Hand & fist
	Fast food options

9 Train to Lose

Don't burn off fat with a candle...
a blowtorch will work quicker.

TRAINING INTENSITY – THE FAT BURNING ZONE?

There was a time when exercisers were urged to train only at low intensities, about 60%-65% of maximum heart rate if they wanted to lose weight. Theoretically, training at this level would use fat rather than carbohydrate as the primary fuel and this would get rid of the fat faster. This heart rate range was known as "The Fat Burning Zone" and the hype surrounding it brought the notion of heart rate monitoring into the mainstream. It turns out that for weight loss, it doesn't really matter what heart rate zone you train in. For weight loss, what matters in the total calories burned. Whether you burn the calories quickly by doing high intensity work or you burn them slowly, it is the net calorie deficit that matters.

The pendulum has swung the other direction and now we see the weight loss benefit of training at higher intensities. The first is time efficiency; you burn calories faster by working harder. If you only have 30 minutes to train, you will burn more calories in that time if you work at a higher heart rate. But that is not all; high intensity work also stimulates the muscles more. Stimulated muscles require energy to adapt and to grow. Increasing the amount of muscle in your body is important if you want to improve body composition.

STRENGTH TRAINING: THE MISSING LINK IN WEIGHT CONTROL

Jim Herkimer, Executive Director of the Sports Conditioning and Rehabilitation Center in Orange, California has worked with many triathletes. More than a physical therapist, Herkimer has an extensive background in exercise physiology and is an athlete himself. He designs strength programs to return triathletes to function following injury, and also to prepare them for the rigors of intense competition. I asked him about strength training for triathletes interested in improving body composition and he explained that strength training is crucial for several reasons:

- It prevents or at least slows the loss of lean mass while you are restricting calories and as you age [73, 74]. Maintaining and increasing lean mass is important because it increases the number of calories you burn at rest (resting metabolic rate). A higher metabolic rate increases your calorie needs and therefore makes it easier to create a calorie deficit so you can lose fat. With more muscle, you will be able to eat more calories and maintain the same weight.

- Strength training also improves body stability and at the same time, optimizes the efficient motion that is necessary for triathlon. This is especially true for movements across all three planes of motion. If you can move better you can train more and harder. Improved muscular stability helps prevent injury that keeps you from training and burning calories.

- Stability and efficient motion is also important to minimize "energy leaks"[75] that is, energy lost by decreased control and excessive movement in the wrong direction. Efficient movement allows higher intensity training which provides greater stimulation of your cardiovascular system. A strong cardio-vascular system allows you to continue to train at high calorie burning and muscle stimulating intensities. Both of these capacities diminish with age but you can hold onto them longer with strength training.

He adds, "Triathletes generally do not reap the benefits of strength training because they are endurance animals. They shy away from the strength training environment because they aren't comfortable there. Consider the background of swimmers, cyclists and runners. Very few of these sports include much strength work."

A triathlete would much rather run for 30 minutes than spend 30 minutes in the gym. I asked Jim which activity is better from a weight management perspective. If an athlete only had 30 minutes for a workout, the answer is simple, "hands down, strength training wins."

But to reap the most benefit, the athlete needs to do the *right kind* of strength work. The emphasis on core strength for triathletes has been both a blessing and a curse. On the one hand, it has encouraged athletes to get into the gym, which is a good thing. The problem is that once there, athletes are doing the wrong exercises.

Standard weight training exercises are done from a stable position, often times seated with back support or lying down completely supported on a bench. From this position, the athlete applies force to move the weight in a single direction (forward, back, up or down). Contrast this to the movements of running, swimming and cycling. Triathlon is very much a tri-planar sport. In order to perform well and prevent injury, the triathlete must be able to generate force simultaneously in three planes of movement, forward and back, across the body, and up and down.

"The advantages of strength training are tremendous," says Herkimer. "Every triathlete should do it, whether they want to improve body composition or not. And it doesn't take much time. Two sessions per week of about 45 minutes is enough."

© Maria.P./Fotolia.com

FUELING GUIDELINES

Triathletes can feel conflicted about eating less to lose weight. The triathlon media pushes all sorts of nutrition products with the promise that fuel is the secret of success in the sport. But if you want to lose weight, you have to create a fuel deficit. How do you fuel properly and create a deficit at the same time? You don't. Take it in two steps; first work on losing fat and getting to your desired body composition, then after you reach your goal you can refocus on performance.

If you train moderately in a slightly depleted state, your performance during that session may suffer and it may take more time to refuel your muscles afterwards (recover), but it is not dangerous. The hand-wringing over this issue is overblown. You do not have to saturate your system with carbohydrates before, during, and after every training session.

The typical guidelines (see Appendix E) recommend eating before, during and after training. The number of calories are based upon body weight, timing and to some degree, exercise intensity.

Here's the problem: According to the guidelines, a 160 pound athlete should eat at least 640 calories before a training session, 300 calories during (2 hour moderate bike ride), and 768 calories afterward. This adds up to a whopping 1,708 calories!

2 hours before the ride:	640 calories (breakfast/lunch)
Intake during the ride:	300 calories
Stage 1 recovery meal:	320 calories
Stage 2 recovery meal:	448 calories (lunch/dinner)
Total training-related intake:	**1,708 calories**

Indeed this athlete will be well-fueled, but if he eats all this, he will have eaten all of his calories for the day (his calorie target from Appendix C is 1,703). He will be one meal short. This will not work, he will be too hungry. Several things can be done to help this athlete and they are discussed below.

TROUBLESHOOTING FOR THE HUNGRY TRIATHLETE

1. ADJUST THE GUIDELINES FOR WEIGHT LOSS

Before Training:
- Eat a calorie conscious meal (in accordance with your calorie target) before your workout. Since you are training at moderate intensity, there should be no digestion problems. Time your meal according to personal preference.

During Training:
- Don't consume *any* calories unless you are going to train longer than 2 hours. You can ride without eating for up to 3 hours at low intensity without ill effects [76].
- Drink water no matter what.
- If your workout is longer than 2-3 hours as above, consume about 280 calories per hour starting at 2 hours [10]. *Don't count these calories in your daily total.* These are *free calories.*

After Training:
- Don't eat a recovery meal *at all* unless you did:
  - a high intensity workout of at least 1 hour, or
  - a low-moderate intensity workout of at least 2 hours.
- Eat about 300-400 calories within 20 minutes-2 hours of finishing. Call it a snack or a meal, but track the food as you would with anything else you eat.

Let's revisit our 160 lb athlete after making these changes:

2 hours before the ride	500 calorie breakfast according to calorie target
Intake during ride	0
Recovery meal/lunch	500 calories according to calorie target
Total training-related intake:	**1000 calories**

(Target calorie intake) 1703 − 1000 = 703 calories left for the rest of the day

This athlete now has 703 calories available to him for the rest of the day.

2. VARY CALORIE INTAKE ACCORDING TO DAILY TRAINING VOLUME

If you are starving after your recovery meal following long workouts, you should eat a little more. You can vary your intake from day to day, as long as you stay within your calorie target for the week. This adds flexibility. Eat more on big training days and less on short days or days off.

3. ADJUST YOUR CALORIE TARGET

Your calorie target should take activity level into account (see Appendix C). The shortcut calorie targets (1,400 for women, 2,000 for men) are based upon a 6 hour training week. If you are training more than that, it is important to do the calculations to come up with a more accurate number.

If you are hungry most of the time, you should adjust your calorie target to slow weight loss a little. There is no need to kill yourself over a small adjustment, especially if doing so keeps you on your program.

If this athlete increased his daily calorie deficit to produce a 1.5 lb loss/week (750 calorie deficit) rather than 2 pounds, he would have a new calorie target of:

2,703 calories to maintain − 750 calorie deficit = 1,953 calories
1,953 (new calorie target) − 1,000 (calories consumed by workout above) = 953 calories

This would allow our athlete another 953 calories for the day.

4. GET THE MOST FROM YOUR TRAINING CALORIES

Another strategy is to get the most satisfaction, taste, mouth feel, etc. from every calorie you consume. There is no shortage of bars, gels, blocks, shakes and drinks to enhance your performance before, during and after training. The varied potions are convenient and concentrated forms of energy which are easy to ingest and digest. They are calorie dense, provide limited variation in texture and taste and have no visual appeal. They are designed to deliver fuel quickly, even when your hunger is diminished. In other words, these fuels deliver a large number of calories when you will least enjoy them.

If you only have few pounds to lose, eliminating these concocted fuels entirely may be the only thing necessary to drop a few pounds. In any case, eating real food will diminish desire for a real meal right after a "recovery bar". Compare the nutritional values and satisfaction levels of the recovery foods in Table 12. Create your own recovery meals to get more food bang for your calorie buck.

Table 12 *Comparison of recovery foods*

Compare foods	Power Bar Chocolate Peanut Butter	Ensure shake	1 C skim milk, whole grain toast, $1/_2$ Tbs peanut butter, tangerine
Calories	240	250	257
Protein grams	10	9	15.1
Carbohydrate grams	45	40	38
Fat grams	3	6	6

You can take this a step further and consume some HCD foods during your recovery meal instead of at other times. This is not to say that you should eat a bunch of junk food, but if you are planning to have some treats, having them after training will lessen their impact. There is evidence that calories consumed in the 2 hour window after training are preferentially stored as glycogen rather than fat [44].

10 The Ironman Trap

> "Like falling in love, there was a chemistry
> that could never be reproduced."
>
> *– Kirk Johnson to the Edge A Man, Death Valley,*
> *and the Mystery of Endurance*

ARE YOU TRAPPED?

When you ask a triathlete, "what is the Ironman Trap?" You get all sorts of answers. One thing is certain; the race has an addictive quality that goes *beyond* the need to do it better and faster next time.

The psychologists would call it obsessive-compulsiveness on the part of the athletes that have intense ego-drives; anthropologists would call it a primitive instinct to travel vast distances in search of food. Physiologists would talk about the humming hormonal sensations set in motion by hours of aerobic training. But the athletes themselves will tell you that being able to eat with abandon is one of the top perks of the Ironman experience. The trap is that the race ends but the eating doesn't.

A month ago Jillian finished her very first Ironman. "During training I was in the very best shape of my life. I was toned, healthy and eating as much as I liked of anything I liked. There seemed no limit to what I could put in my mouth. Really, no matter how much I ate, I still lost a little weight each week, so I kept eating."

She continues, "Now it is time to pay the piper. I realize that this can't continue and I'm going to have to reduce my intake back to normal. But the problem is that I'm not like normal people, I have very little self-control when it comes to eating. Whatever self-control I had, I forgot during my training. What the heck is normal? I'm going to have to figure it out all over again."

The way to stay out of the Ironman Trap is to hold on to the weight-conscious habits that served you well before you started your Ironman training. That is easier said than done. When your time is at a premium it is easy to forego planning related to food and grab whatever is available and when are exceptionally tired, food helps you recover emotionally from the stress of training.

Remember your biology is against you as far as weight is concerned. An arduous undertaking like preparing for an Ironman opens the door for your natural tendencies to sneak back in and take hold. Your brain is engaged with surviving the training load and sustaining a functional life with work and family.

It is important to maintain healthy eating habits during IM training. Even though you can get away with slacking off, it is better not to.

HOW TO AVOID THE TRAP

Ironman training is not the time to focus on weight loss. Triathletes that want to lose weight will be better served if they focus on weight loss at another time. The main goal of this chapter is to keep Ironman Triathletes from gaining weight or from developing a host of bad habits they will have to unlearn when the event is over.

There are two ways to avoid the trap:
1. Instead of becoming a constant eating machine, use controlled recovery meals to provide the extra calories you need. Keep the rest of your eating in check.
2. Use a modified version of the tools for success.

DON'T BECOME AN EATING MACHINE

Training for an Ironman can double the training volume from maintenance level, but it *should not double your calorie intake*. On average, your daily calorie needs will only increase by about 300 calories a day (see Appendix E). Consume those extra calories is in your recovery meals. Eat normally the rest of the time. This will keep you from getting into the habit of eating extra calories throughout the day.

Fueling during training sessions:
Fueling during your sessions is vital. You need the energy and you need to experiment for race day. An effective, tested fueling plan is crucial to Ironman success. There is no merit to under-fueling during training sessions so you can lose weight. The training volumes are too large and persistent.

In Chapter 9 I told you to consume fuel only for training sessions exceeding 2 hours. In the case of IM training, things are different. In sessions lasting longer than 2 *continuous hours* you should *start consuming about 280 calories per hour immediately*, and continue for the entire session.

It you have multiple sessions shorter than 2 continuous hours each with a few hours between, do not require fuel *during* each session.

Recovery Meals:
The way to keep a lid on your total calorie intake is to control and get the most from recovery meals. Returning home after a 6-hour training session without knowing what to eat first is a recipe for disaster.

When you train for an Ironman, the calories in your recovery meal should reflect the length of your training session. You can use the chart (Table 16) in Appendix C to estimate calorie needs or you can estimate about 350 recovery calories for every hour exceeding 2 hours of continuous training. Remember that you will have already consumed about 280 calories per hour *during* those longer sessions.

A recovery meal after a 4 hr session = 4 hrs x 350 calories/hr = 1400 calories

What if you train in multiple sessions? If the total training time for the day will exceed 2 hours, you should have a recovery meal (350 calories per hour) after each session. Eat within 20 minutes and no more than 2 hours after each session.

Planning and if convenient, preparing recovery meals ahead of time should be part of your training routine. It will ultimately save you time and stress. Emphasize real, solid food in favor of prepackaged gels, bars, etc. This will provide more eating satisfaction.

The Controlled Feast:
The controlled feast is the recovery meal reserved for your longest training session each week.

The feast should be mostly healthy food that is packed with nutrients. Include colorful vegetables, fruits and protein, but prepare it the way you like it. This is your chance to eat flavorful sauces and fattier cuts of meat.

The feast is special because it is your chance to eat some of the High Calorie Density foods you crave, but usually limit like ice cream, chocolate, pork ribs, salad dressing, creamy sauces, cheese, pizza or chips.

A well orchestrated recovery feast should replace the largest meal of the day and it will support your recovery psychologically and physically.

The feast will only be as good as you make it so plan ahead. You can cook it yourself, or make it the big family meal. It can be take-out food, drive-thru, your favorite restaurant or pizza delivery. The key is that is what you really *want*.

MODIFY THE TOOLS FOR SUCCESS

Most of the tools described in Chapter 9 will remain useful when you are training for an Ironman. Table 13 lists the tools and some comments about applying them to the Ironman experience.

GETTING BACK TO NORMAL

When the dust has cleared and you are an Ironman for the first or the fifteenth time, you will have a few months to mourn the end of your grand adventure and recalibrate your life. Go back to the skills and the tools that have helped you. It's like falling off a horse; you must get back on right away. The sooner you re-establish normal eating patterns, the better off you will be.

Table 13 *Applying the tools for success to Ironman training*

Tool	Comments for Ironman training
Daily Practice	Focus on IM performance.
Accountability	You may not have time to attend weekly meetings
Acknowledge success	Use IM training goals as measures of success.
Modify habits	Probably no time for this.
Pay attention to hunger	You may not have time to eat only when hungry.
Record weight	Expect large fluctuations.
Renew motivation	Focus on IM performance, not weight loss.
Throw it out	Stick with this.
Time between meals	Your mealtimes will depend on training schedule.
Track what you eat	Save time by tracking food in the same place and at the same time you track your training.
Train to maintain	Forget this one. Train to perform.
Social Tools	
Attitude	Should be even better now that you are training for an IM.
Personal support	You will need this more than ever for IM training.
Say "No thanks"	Stay strong on this.
Social occasions	You won't have time for much of this.
Stop sampling	Continue this.
Weight-related support	You may not have time to socialize or attend meetings
Hunger Tools	
Avoid alcohol	Stick to this.
Control daily treats	Stick to this.
Control food variety	Continue this.
Eat protein	Yes
Have access to safe snacks	Avoid the temptation of junk food snacks in the house. Keep quality snacks in your car and office.
Leftovers for later	This will be very helpful.
Make recipes	Helpful if you have time.
Tools for dining out	
Avoid fat	Continue this.
Go green	Continue this.
Hand & fist	Continue this.
Fast food options	Continue this.

PART 5 – MINDSET

11 Success Stories

Triathlon changes the context of your existence –
and adds to the stuff in your garage.

MATT LIETO: IN THE FAST LANE

In 1999 Matt Lieto was Chris Lieto's hefty little brother, there in Kona to cheer Chris. Matt weighed 250 lbs, about 70 pounds more than he does today. As he worked an aid station handing water to Ironman athletes, he had an epiphany.

"It was amazing! These beasts that had already swam and ridden for hours and now were running by almost too fast for me to get them their much needed water. I wasn't able to run fast enough to keep up with them even for more than 20 feet."

"I spent the rest of the day, and up until midnight on the finish line, watching all the makes and models come across. Young, old, fast, slow, skinny, chubby, fresh and worked. Needless to say, I was inspired. If a 78-year-old man bent over by a locked-up back can do this, I can at least get off my butt and do something. ANYTHING!"

"I felt the Ironman was an impossible feat and yet I saw people achieve it. My impossible feat at the time was to finally lose the weight."

He decided to change his life. At the time, he did not have a clear vision of how he wanted life to be, he just knew he wanted to be a participant in it. He was tired of sitting on the sidelines hating himself. His was a journey to happiness and self-acceptance. No more food for comfort. Food was for fuel only.

Matt did two things when he returned to his college campus: He changed his eating and he discovered an activity he loved. His food plan was simple; eat like a king at breakfast, a prince at lunch and a pauper at dinner. This is what a typical food day looked like for Matt:

Breakfast:	4-5 egg whites in an omelet, toast and cereal
Lunch:	Sandwich and fruit or pretzels
Dinner:	Grilled vegetables and tofu

He followed some other rules too:
- Only fruit for snacks
- Lots of vegetables
- No processed food (anything in a box or packaged)
- No fatty goods
- Lots of water
- No sweets

At the same time, he was enticed by a local skateboarding park and found there a passion for outdoor fun that he could do for several hours a day. "The weight loss happened so quickly and somewhat without my noticing the extent of my loss. I didn't really have any bad patches in that time. I was focused on my dedication to change and in the process, felt so much better that change came easily. I was so immersed in the joy of being truly active that I just kept rolling with it because it felt so good."

"I didn't tell my family what was happening until I came home." His mom was understandably floored and thought he was ill. "I can't blame her as her eternally chubby son had lost 75 lbs in a few months." He went from "sucking into size 38's to 32's" in 5 months. He lost weight very quickly, about 4 pounds per week.

The weight loss ignited his desire to take on new outdoor challenges. He started tentatively and with each success his confidence grew. He decided to try a triathlon and started to train for the Wildflower Olympic distance. He achieved his time goal there, then made big goals for how he would place in the coming 2 years. He achieved those goals and it felt like his life was turning around. He was becoming a happy-go-lucky guy and his attitude about life changed.

His Brother, Chris is 7 years older. Chris was just breaking through as a professional triathlete with his first win at Wisconsin when Matt started to become competitive in his own right. Chris made the learning curve easy for Matt. Their shared interest in triathlon brought them together. Neither brother knew where the sport would take them. Matt's attitude was "If Chris can do it, maybe I can too," so it has been a parallel journey with Chris a few years ahead.

Matt is now also a professional triathlete. He believes he can win Ironman races and be the best in the sport. He keeps reminding himself, "I AM one of those athletes and I CAN win."

"I don't push the low body fat as much as some other athletes in the sport. Based on experience, my performance suffers if I am on the 'razors edge.' I probably carry 1-2% more fat than a lot of my competitors, but I depend on my strength to compensate. And I never forget that I am down from 250 so 170 is good enough for me!!"

"I find that as a society, we snack so much we are adding meals that we don't need. I know many people believe in eating many meals throughout the day and keeping the metabolism high. I think this can work, but only with small ones, not 3 big meals with some extra ones thrown in. We simply don't need that many calories in a normal day."

SCOTT REINVENTED HIMSELF

Scott is considering cosmetic surgery to remove the extra skin that he carries following his 100 pound weight loss. Here is his story ...

"In the course of a month I quit drinking, quit drugging and joined AA.

I started losing weight after I quit drinking. Making improvements to my health became central in my mind because I had already taken the biggest step.

I tried to avoid snacking very much, ate only healthy foods (no fast food, not too many processed foods, no desserts, no late-night snacking), and quit smoking, and started exercising a lot. It's nearly impossible for me to control my appetite but I am not afraid to sweat.

The first half of the weight loss was from the changes I made in my eating and plenty of exercise on treadmills/walk/running/cycling/etc. When I was about 250 lbs a friend of mine told me I should do a 5K; I did my first the next day. After that, a friend dared me to do a sprint tri that was in about a month. I was scared but I just signed up, knowing I could easily just put it off in fear and never even try. Having already committed, I was motivated to step up the training to just be able to finish and then the weight really started to fall off; I went from 250 lb to 235 in about a month.

I signed up for more triathlons and at first the improvements come fast and were significant. I was dropping my times every 5K, triathlon and bike race. Weight was coming off without much effort. I signed up for more ambitious races such as 5 milers, lock's, Olympic triathlons, half-marathons and marathons, and the progression kept providing new goals and challenges that kept me training harder and harder. I love the variety that triathlon affords me. With the training that each sport entails, I can never get bored. When I injure an Achilles (easy to do running when you are really overweight), I can focus on swimming or cycling.

It was like flipping a switch. Weight loss for me was never about self-will, it wasn't about whether I had a little ice cream or not, it was about the progress?it was the result of a psychic change. When you are in the zone, it isn't hard. When you aren't, it's nearly impossible. I wish I could explain that better but I'm sure others who have lost the amount of weight I have would tell you something similar.

The "alcohol issue" was more than that, it was a way of life. AA teaches you that "alcohol is but a symptom of the problem"; it is a spiritual and emotional problem that causes one to drink rather than simply a physical addiction (although that is also true). I used alcohol and drugs to treat an emptiness in my life as well as anxiety. Eventually the alcohol and drugs go from being your friend to your master. In short, this is when I finally was able to surrender and recover.

I had nothing to fill the void that was left by giving-up alcohol. First, all of a sudden I had 6-8 hours in the day to fill. Second, I had to deal with all the chaos that I had wrought in my life?chemical withdrawal, loss of friends, repercussions at work, having become morbidly obese, etc. I also needed the stress reduction from regular exercise.

I had to give up the ?friends? I had as an addict, so I was left with no one. Triathlon eventually gave me a lot of new friends who shared a common hobby.

One friend I had made in AA was an Ironman; he was inspirational and also taught me that exercise was vital to emotional health and one of the keys to filling that emptiness inside of me. Triathlon was an area where I could see immediate progress in my life and I needed that boost.

I was taught to "stick with the winners," because you tend to aspire to become the ones who you associate with. People who can deny themselves to the point of finishing an event such as an Ironman are the type of people I admire and having them in my circle of friends is inspirational."

Success us everywhere if you look for it. The world is full of triathletes that have found this sport as vehicle for change in their lives. Whether weight loss is fast or slow, it comes on the heels of an inspired commitment to change. As Kevin Shaw, 105 pounds lighter says, "I don't feel the need to race all the time as this is a lifestyle for me. *Almost as if I don't really ever want to cross the finish line.*"

12 Motivation

You must be strong enough, brave enough and
wise enough to be true to yourself.

MOVE AWAY FROM PAIN

DISSATISFACTION

Looks matter. Having the right weight and shape and being fit are important attributes in our culture [77]. Like it or not, self-management, hard work, delay of gratification and impulse control are qualities projected onto people with the right body [78]. One of the most painful aspects of being overweight is what it says about you, whether those things are true or not. In our culture, being overweight conveys a message of poor discipline and laziness. Being fit, training hard and having a weight problem is like being at war with yourself. The world can see that you are disciplined enough to train but it is obvious that you eat too much. Don't get me wrong, everyone is imperfect and of the many things that can be wrong in a person's life, overeating is puny compared to the other horrors people suffer through. Everyone has personal issues and appearance isn't everything. That said, it is embarrassing to have your weakness displayed so obviously for the world to see, especially when you put yourself out there as a triathlete. Your weight is something you can change, so why suffer with it?

Self-consciousness spoils everything. Every time you go for a run you wear a shirt to cover up, or you always wear something over your swimsuit to hide your rear end. There is nothing wrong with modesty, but that little voice in your head is telling you "this isn't fair, I want to feel good about my body – I work hard enough at it." It is that little voice that brings the pain. And you know what? There is nothing you can do to squelch it. You can spend thousands of dollars on psychotherapy to 'reframe' your self-concept but it is all smoke and mirrors. Losing weight improves body image much more effectively than psychological treatment does [79]. You have to lose the weight so that you can be satisfied with yourself.

You have to change to overcome this pain, but change is difficult. It is so difficult that for the most part, you will only do it when things get so bad you can't stand it anymore.

Are you there yet?

TRIGGERING EVENTS

The National Weight Control Registry (NWCR) tracks over 5,000 individuals who have lost significant amounts of weight and kept it off for long periods of time. They publish research on a regular basis in scientific journals and on their website, *www.nwcr.ws*.

A recent NWCR study revealed that 83% of successful weight losers reported a triggering event leading to their weight loss. A successful weight loser is defined as someone that has lost more than 10% of their highest weight and has kept it off for a year or more.

The most common trigger was a health threat, either a warning from their doctor or the death of a family member caused by an obesity-related problem. Reaching an all time high in weight, and seeing an unflattering photo or seeing their own reflection in the mirror are also common triggers [80].

Dan was motivated by a medical trigger. "I didn't want the doctor telling me I would not live to see 35." Eric was unhappy at 260 lbs. "It took a couple pictures from racing last season to really hit home the fact that I was fat. I carry it well since it disperses evenly but I had two freaking chins. *Unacceptable*."

"My daughter was the motivation for me," says Kevin. "One time we were watching TV and there was a show about obese people and my daughter told me that my belly looked like the guy on TV. The guy weighed over 600 pounds. This got me thinking about how you see yourself versus how others see you. I was not on the same scale (no pun intended) as the guy on TV, but I certainly had extra body fat hanging all over me. The second event was similar... we were driving in the car and we passed a large man riding a bicycle. My daughter said that he looked like me when I ride my bike. I did not think I looked like that however I probably did. These comments are what made me decide to get in shape and find something that would allow me to stay in shape for a lifetime."

Avoiding pain is the primary fuel for the decision to lose weight. Addicts call it "hitting bottom," a level of suffering so deep and awful that it triggers a fundamental shift in your thinking. You can set the trigger on your own weight loss by getting your emotions involved.

Trigger exercise

Make a list of every reason you can think of that being at your current weight is bad, painful, unpleasant, unmotivating. It's OK to start with health reasons, but don't stop there. Write down the ugly stuff that comes to mind when you see yourself overeating, the things you feel when you are at a race and thinner people are passing you.

When you are out in the world do others see you as an athlete? or just another overweight person that has given their life to convenience foods and sloth? Do you look younger than you are, or much older? Does failing at weight control again and again make you feel stupid, undisciplined, weak, slow? Go ahead, let it all hang out. Cry it out if you must. Find that darkness and dive in.

Acknowledge what your weight problem cost your soul.

FEEL THE PULL OF SUCCESS

"Success is not the result of spontaneous combustion.
You must set yourself on fire."

– Reggie Leach

IMAGINE SUCCESS

Now that you have gotten yourself good and depressed, work on the flip side. Imagine how life will be *without* a persistent weight problem.

Imagine success

- *How much faster would you be if you were lean?*
- *What is appealing about looking lean and athletic?*
- *What do you think when you see an exceptionally fit man or woman walking down the street? What characteristics do you ascribe to them? Discipline, liveliness, intelligence?*
- *What would it feel like to be one of those fit people for the rest of your life?*
- *How great would it be to go running without a shirt, or to wear your bikini without shame?*
- *What would it be like to look like the athlete you know you are? How will being fit impact your children? What example will you set?*
- *Imagine knowing that you are finally in control of your food.*
- *What will it be like to wear your body with pride?*
- *Bathe yourself in the sensation of your smallest jeans feeling loose.*
- *Imagine muscle definition in your arms, going sleeveless, six pack anyone?*

The dream is important. It activates the brain. Dream of leanness all the time. Looks matter to us so much that our bodies can change to fulfill our dreams.

A 1992 study demonstrated the power of imagination. Subjects were instructed to focus on lifting weights with a particular finger over a period of time. One group actually exercised the finger, another only imagined doing it. After a few weeks the group that had actually exercised the finger increased muscular strength by 30%. But those that only imagined doing it increased their strength by 22% [81].

All it takes is the same patience and persistence you apply to your training. *Extend the athletic drive that you already possess.*

LOOKS OR SPEED?

This exercise will help you define why you want you be lean. Is it looks you are after, or speed?

If you had to choose between looking fast or being fast for the rest of your life, what would you choose?

Some of the benefits of looking fast are relief from weight management issues, the intimidation factor at races, the motivation that comes from looking fit and athletic all the time, wearing smaller clothes, the health benefits of being lean, not "having" to train hard to maintain your look. Looking fast does not preclude you from working to get faster, so you can still set and achieve goals. But if you choose this option, you will never qualify for Kona and will never be on the podium. Hmm... think about it.

What about *being* fast instead? You would not have to train very hard and your medal box would be overflowing. You could enjoy the stunned looks on the faces of all the skinny guys and gals as you zoom by them in races. You could shock co-workers when you tell them you actually *won* a triathlon in spite of the extra pounds you are carrying. Maybe you could turn pro?

The answer to this question will tell you plenty about what motivates and what will make you happy in the long term.

THE SUCCESS CYCLE

It is important to give successful weight loss a meaning that empowers you. Control over your own actions is the only power you have. You can't control others or the outside world, but if you are confident that you can control yourself, you can manage anything. You will know that nothing will throw you off the weight loss track. The certainty of knowing you will achieve your goal brings serenity to your life. Positive experiences, thoughts and actions build on each other, creating a cycle of success (see Figure 5).

Figure 5 *Success Cycle*

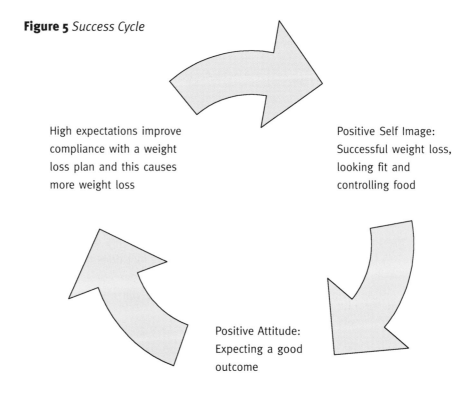

High expectations improve compliance with a weight loss plan and this causes more weight loss

Positive Self Image: Successful weight loss, looking fit and controlling food

Positive Attitude: Expecting a good outcome

Kevin found that focusing on multiple sports was a key for him. Having a bad day or two in one discipline did not affect the other two. He could always find something to do and could focus on "the positive things in terms of speed or perceived effort. This turned into a very positive tool both physically and mentally. As my times for certain activities started to decrease, this was motivation to work harder, which burned more calories, which translated into more weight loss. The lower weight was less resistance that allowed me to move faster. As this was happening I started to really focus on my diet..."

Results work. When things start to come together, you will feel the power. That power will drive you to more success and before you know it, your life will become exceptional.

ARRIVAL

Once you achieve your Better Than Ever weight, your life will already be different. The changes come gradually and just getting there will show that you are up to the task. As body fat stores are reduced, your appetite will go down. It truly does get easier [84]. But having arrived at the finish, you will see that you have arrived at the beginning of a new life.

You will return, from time to time, to your food log and the tools that have helped you. You will not be perfect about every aspect of eating and nutrition, but you will know what you can and what you can't get away with.

You might feel a little unsteady at first, like the new you on the outside is someone other than the old you lurking inside. This is normal. It highlights the importance of setting a goal that lasts a lifetime. *Losing weight is changing your identity* and it takes time to adjust. It takes time for you to come to recognize that the image in the mirror is you. It will also take a few years before your friends and family accept that this new you is permanent.

Having overcome your food demons, you will gain confidence that will grow decision by decision, day by day. Maintaining weight loss is a tremendous challenge but for triathletes it is much easier because there is no need to "sell" you on exercise.

Interest and enjoyment of exercise plays a more important role in long term weight management than in the initial stages of weight loss, so train your heart out [85]. Training is a built-in success machine offering constant positive feedback for maintaining your goal weight.

Your new weight will soon become your normal weight because:
1. You train regularly year round.
2. You now look forward to race photos.
3. Your wardrobe fits you at this size, not the old size.
4. You are truly happy with yourself now.
5. You have gotten faster and have plans to get faster still.
6. You have deeply ingrained habits that will help you stay lean.
7. You always know what you weigh and monitor your body composition closely so you can act quickly if the scale creeps up a few pounds.
8. You will have practiced many strategies for managing temptation, overcoming setbacks, making good choices and staying motivated.

According to the National Weight Control Registry, those that successfully maintain weight loss have certain things in common:
- The single best predictor of successful maintenance is reaching the 2 year mark. After that, it becomes progressively easier to maintain weight loss.
- Less out of control eating.
- At least 1 hour per day of exercise.
- Satisfaction from exercise in and of itself, high motivation to exercise and feeling competent at the activity.
- Lower levels of depression [85].
- Consistent food intake in spite of holidays, weekends and travel [83].

When you reach your weight loss anniversary, you can register at www.NWCR.WS and become one of their research subjects. Mark your calendar.

BECOME A MENTAL MASTER

Learning occurs in stages. The so called, "conscious competence model" illustrates the process as a series of steps:

Step 1: Unconscious Incompetence –
> A person in this stage eats with abandon all the time, unconcerned about his weight. An athlete that has mastered his weight will never return to this step, he knows too much.

Step 2: Conscious Incompetence –
> An athlete at this stage knows he would perform better if he paid attention to food, but he doesn't want to mess with it. This is the most painful stage psychologically. People in this stage complain about lacking motivation, time or other resources to address the problem. Such a person knows about calories and weight loss but doesn't take action to change.

> When an athlete masters her weight, she will rarely occupy this step. If she does, it will only be for a meal or two.

Step 3: Conscious Competence –
> Athletes at this stage are following a plan and are actively losing weight. They make the right choices and they do the things that will lead them to their goals, but it's a daily struggle. This is the stage where the athletes need resources like the tools in Chapter 8 to get through the day.

> Athletes that have mastered their weight spend progressively less time at this stage, but never leave it entirely. A few days at this stage effectively channels them back to Step 4.

Step 4: Unconscious Competence –
> At this stage, athletes eat well without really having to think about it. The principles of effective eating and the tools to execute them have become second nature. Stage 4 is the goal. Triathletes that have mastered their weight are here most of the time. They perceive themselves and the world around them in a way that reinforces their competence with food.

Just as triathlon was once an activity, in time it became part of you. The same is true with weight management. Constant practice propels you to Stage 4. What used to be an effort gets easier and eventually it all feels normal. At some point your self-image will merge with your lean body and you will have achieved mastery.

Focus is the key. Successful athletes use a variety of mental strategies to maximize their performance. These strategies all begin with directing focus where they want it to be. The longer the race, the longer you must sustain focus.

Managing your weight *for the rest of your life* requires sustaining focus longer than any race. View weight management as a mental challenge. Keep focused on images that drive you forward and ignore the ones that get in your way.

Weight control is a path to mental mastery. It is not frivolous vanity. It requires superior personal management skills that few possess. Focus, persist and you will prevail.

WEIGHT MANAGEMENT FOR TRIATHLETES

13 Action

Don't say......DO!

– H.G. Loos

DECIDE

The back and forth agony of half-hearted resolutions and little failures saps your spirit and makes your life pretty bleak. Repeated failure is stressful. It weakens self-confidence and motivation [85].

> **Decide:** To bring to a definitive end (Merriam Webster Online Dictionary 2009)

You have to decide; not lean toward, not intend, not wish for. You simply must decide to do whatever it takes to reach your weight goal and stay there for life because you are unwilling to put up with things the way they are for one more minute. You won't waste one more day of your life in this funk, this anger, this sadness that you have allowed. Failing is not an option because your self-respect is tied up into it.

Once you decide, you are set free, you are in motion. Motivation is fuel. The act of deciding lights the match. It will illuminate your path.

Once Scott decided to lose weight, "it was like flipping a switch. Weight loss for me was never about self-will, it was not about having a little ice cream, it was about the progress, it was the result of a psychic change. When you are in the zone, it isn't hard: When you aren't, it is next to impossible."

How do you get into the "zone?" You decide. Once you decide, the switch is "On" and all that is left is to act.

ACT NOW

No, you will not start your "diet" tomorrow! Delaying action is a way to avoid it. You are going to change the way you eat for the rest of your life, so you might as well start now. If you are in the proper state of mind, you are ready to get on with it now.

> "Only put off till tomorrow what you are willing to die having left undone."
>
> – *Picasso*

PERSIST

Making changes will be uncomfortable at times, and you have to accept some tedium and discomfort. Remember the first time you went for a run after a layoff? It took forever to find your shoes, your iPod was dead, and you couldn't remember how to use your heart rate monitor. But you didn't give up. You may have been disorganized, but you managed to get your stuff together and you got out the door. After that, it was easy.

Starting a new weight loss plan is even worse, I won't lie. There is a tendency to want every aspect of your plan to be lined up before you start. Don't make it so difficult. Just get started. You won't have it all together on the first day, but you will have it eventually. Be willing to do what is required.

Choose a tracking method from Chapter 6 and aim for your calorie target every day. Accept and embrace having to learn new things. Invest in the process. Now that you have decided, you are on your way. Just put one foot in front of the other and you will be fine.

When circumstances make this new plan difficult, work through it. When people seem to stand in your way, go around them.

THROW AWAY THE KEY

As you progress, get rid of the clothes that are too big for you. Get rid of them *right away*. It is OK to keep something tucked away as a memento, but don't keep a duplicate wardrobe in a larger size, just in case. Don't give yourself that option. Deciding means putting the past behind you, permanently.

Since you are going to be slimmer in a few weeks, sign up for a race in the near future. You know that you will be leaner and maybe even faster. Maintenance level training may not improve your speed but it will keep you fit enough to participate. Buy the snappy tri outfit you plan to fit into and hang it in an obvious place that you see every day.

Plan an "A" priority race for a few months after you expect to reach your goal. Get the gear you need. Find the training plan to use when you reach your goal. How much faster will you be? Box yourself into success at every opportunity

BE TENACIOUS

Tenacity: Te-nac-i-ty: *noun* Application, backbone, chutzpah, clock, courage, determination, doggedness, firmness, grit, guts, heart, inflexibility, intestinal fortitude, moxie, nerve, obstinacy, perseverance, persistence, resoluteness, resolution, resolve, spunk, starch, staunchness, steadfastness, stick-to-itiveness, stomach, strength of purpose, true grit, what it takes [86].

Tenacity is a toughness in sprit that is off-putting to some. It says, "Don't mess with me." There will be times during your quest when others will be surprised or even offended by your refusal to 'be reasonable" to "give in" or have "just one taste" of this or that. I hate to say it, but some of the people you know and love will be threatened by your commitment to change, others will be puzzled. They don't want you to fail, but they expect it. Be prepared for it and keep moving forward with your plan.

Triathletes are bombarded with information at every turn. There is considerable opportunity to get sidetracked with the latest training plan or nutritional approach. If you change directions willy-nilly every time you get a new online newsletter or triathlon magazine, you won't get anywhere but frustrated. Jumping around from plan to plan will get you nowhere. Stick to this plan.

MAKE WEIGHT LOSS THE PRIORITY

"Losing weight and maintaining a good training diet?it seems diametrically opposed. On the one hand I'm trying to build up my body and give it enough nutrients to train, but then I find I'm not getting any leaner if I don't restrict my diet," says Stephanie.

Make losing weight and reaching your Better Than Ever goal more important (right now) than performing well. It is also more important than pleasing all of the other people in your life all of the time. This does not mean that you become selfish and rude. It means that you find a way to do what needs to be done, even if it is something new or requires some negotiating with people who are important to you.

Many of the situations that can cause conflict are discussed in Chapter 8. You have the tools to deal with them.

STOP WHINING

Avoid wishy-washy words like "struggling," "trying" or "wanting". Wimpy words undermine resolve.

Complainers are looking for permission to fail. Let them. Resist the urge to placate. This only drags you into the muck. Be a rock. Everything you say with regard to this issue must exude optimistic certainty in your success

> **"I let negativity roll off me like water off a duck's back.
> If it's not positive, I didn't hear it."**
>
> *– George Foreman*

LAUGH

Grown-ups trying to extract themselves from wetsuits that won't let go... spending an extra $100 to save 1 oz on your bike pedals... a middle-aged lawyer busting her butt to look better in spandex shorts than her 20 year-old secretary. Triathlon is sort of funny. How about losing 15 pounds so you can take a few minutes off a day-long Ironman race? In the scheme of things, no one cares about all this as much as you do. Allow yourself the luxury of a good laugh at this sport and at your fixation on it... it is, after all, just for fun... right? But it is SERIOUS fun and losing weight will make it even more so. Enjoy the process. Enjoy your progress.

CELEBRATE PROGRESS

Don't forget to acknowledge your progress. It you join a commercial weight loss program, you will get plenty of pats on the back but it is important to get into the habit of congratulating yourself too. Once you reach your goal and the world no longer notices the change in you, there will be only one person that will appreciate how far you have come and that is you.

Instead of another doomed new year's resolution, use the holiday to reinforce your mastery over food. Remembering what motivated you to change and giving yourself credit for your accomplishment will help you sustain it. You don't have to throw a party, but find a way to celebrate your accomplishment every year.

The satisfaction that will come from sustaining your ideal weight will make your best race performance pale in comparison. You display your race medals, what can you do to acknowledge your weight management success?

© Unspecified/fotolia.com

14 Weight Divisions

So if I'm out there riding with you,
and you think you're a bad-ass cyclist,
a hammer, a machine, and you're feeling
all smug about yourself because you're a few hundred yards
ahead of me on the long, long hill,
let me tell you, buddy,
if I can see you on the road ahead of me,
if I'm anywhere close to you,
I'm really kicking your ass.

– Mike Magnuson, Heft on Wheels: A Field Guide to Doing a 180.

BIG OR FAT?

Admit it. If they called it the fat division, it wouldn't have much appeal. In this increasingly overweight world these athletes are in some circles, average. But in triathlon, they are heavyweights. Triathlon is a planet unto itself, with it's own definitions and prejudices and one of them is a troubled relationship with weight divisions.

LARGE TRIATHLETES CAN'T WIN

The prejudice against weight division athletes stems from the notion that an overweight athlete should not get special treatment. His weight is within his control and if he wants to be faster, he should lose weight. Opponents say you don't have to be lean to be fit and overweight athletes should be allowed to race against likeminded others in their own division. Both views leave the tall, muscular but lean athlete out in the cold. Such an athlete suffers a weight disadvantage even though he is lean. If he races as a Clydesdale he is cheating. If he races and wins in his age group, he is stealing the prize from a normal sized athlete.

Looking at the history of weight divisions fails to shed much light on this central issue. To say that weight division athletes are a homogeneous group is ridiculous. But it is what they have in common, rather than their differences, that defines the class. What they have in common is weight, and weight slows you down.

HISTORY

The weight class movement originated and persists in running events. In the early 1980's, Joe Law devised the weight division concept based upon a statistical model he developed. It showed that above 160 pounds, running times drop dramatically. In an attempt to even the playing field in running events, he founded the Clydesdale Runner's Association. This organization promoted the inclusion of weight classes in running events.

Les Smith, race director of the Portland Marathon, was also onto the concept and in 1984, was probably the first to include weight divisions in such an event. He recalls taking advantage of a promotional opportunity which included a visit by Ed McMann of the *Johnny Carson Show*. Says Smith, "He was in town for a promotion with Budweiser and the Clydesdale horses so we grabbed at this and had some pictures taken with him with some of our "big" athletic men and women." Smith and the Portland Marathon continue to support the movement.

Organizations like The USA Clydesdale and Filly Racing Federation (USACFRF), and the Chicago Area Runners Association (CARA) embraced the weight division concept. CARA members compete in a circuit and are ranked according to their weight/age division over the season.

The RunBig organization was founded in 2000 by Buck Hales, promoting weight divisions in triathlons and running events. These groups were born in the Chicago area. CARA is the only one that remains active.

POLITICS

"The original and sole purpose of Team Clydesdale International (TCI), founded in 1996, was to gain recognition of weight classes at the Ironman World Championships in Kona," says founder, Guy East, Sr. At the time, it was the only nationally organized body supporting weight class competition for triathletes.

Unfortunately, the lobbying efforts of TCI failed. Then president of the WTC, the owner the Ironman brand said "until the division can standardize, unify and globalize, there will never be serious consideration for WTC to expand."

"So," says East, "our small band of Clydes decided to change our mission statement which is now, "to educate and encourage fitness, camaraderie and competition among large athletes."

Even though weight classes never made it to Kona, North America Sports recognized them in its Ironman and 70.3 events through 2008. They gave awards to the top 3 finishers in the weight divisions and to the top 4 finishers in the age-groups.

In 2009, WTC eliminated weight divisions entirely from their events. They are unresponsive to inquiries. East thinks they made the move for financial reasons. He admits the TCI membership has dwindled. WTC has decided that the egg must come before the chicken on this issue. Indeed, if WTC announced that Kona slots would be awarded to weight divisions there would be a gigantic jump in weight-class participation. The level of competition would tighten considerably. The divisions would be well populated, competitive and the objections would probably disappear.

Says Buck Hales of RunBig, "Unfortunately the Clydesdale movement has been dominated by a handful of leaders whose personalities dictated the direction each regional entity took. There is still tremendous interest in Clydesdale racing and more and more middle and back of the pack runners of size are attracted to the competition, but the lack of cooperative leadership has hurt the establishment and acceptance of the divisions."

In spite of poor organization, "15-18% of the USAT member population are Clydesdales. 10% of that number are Athena. As long as Team Clydesdale speaks for their constituents, our members will find value and benefit in associating." Says East. TCI continues to advertise in magazines, but the emphasis on the website is racing wheels and workout videos. Logo-printed triathlon clothing is no longer available.

PARTICIPATION

"Women seem to be at odds with each other about what the weight standards should be for Athenas," says East. USAT recognizes a 150 lb standard but race directors are known to use weights as low as 140, and up to 160 pounds as minimums to race as an Athena.

Says Kelly, "I don't care what the scale says. I care about being the best athlete I can be and if that puts me into the Athena category, great. I have been passed by athletes of all shapes and sizes and I have learned that you can't judge ability or spirit by body size."

Women with this outlook are in the minority. No matter what the weight standard, the Athena divisions are drastically under-populated. A typical race usually attracts about a dozen Athenas. As varied as the minimum weights are, it is not the size requirement that limits the participation. Look around and at any race at least 25 % of the women are heavy enough to race as Athenas. The problem is they don't want to.

When researchers at the University of Dayton gathered 5K participants for their study comparing performances of lighter vs. heavier runners, they *could not find one woman willing to participate in the study* (see below). Women don't want to get on the scale.

At least for now, women would rather keep their weight a "secret" than enjoy the more favorable odds of winning in the Athena division. Says a newbie, "I was afraid to race as an Athena because I thought I would have to get on the scale to accept my award if I won".

Men are not so reluctant. For men, big is good, winning is good and even being compared to a draft horse is good. Clydesdale divisions are very competitive and often have more participants than some of the age-groups. Men focused on performance see that competing with peers makes the race a more accurate measure of their ability and thus, a better race.

WHY DOES TRIATHLON NEED WEIGHT DIVISIONS?

The age-group concept is so ingrained that it is never questioned, but in the early 70's, age divisions did not exist. Awards were given to the top 5 or 10 runners that crossed the line. The age-group concept came about when the scientific community recognized that aerobic capacity diminishes with age. Proponents of the weight division concept hope that weight divisions will ultimately become standard practice as well. There is plenty of evidence that weight is a disadvantage in running.

THE CLYDESDALE HANDICAP

Drs. Vanderburgh and Laubach at the University of Dayton studied the influence of body size on running. Their studies have confirmed a 15-20% penalty against heavier runners when using VO_{2max} as a predictor of running speed [87]. This study was limited to men because no women were willing to participate in the study.

In 2007, they developed a size-based handicapping formula for use in 5K running races. As part of their work, they determined the ideal body size for 5K runners. The top 30 male and female runners in the world were used as standards. The ideal female runner is 25 years and weighs 110 lbs. The ideal male is 26 years old and 143 pounds. The further away you are from this ideal, the slower you run.

Validation studies have confirmed what larger runners have said all along; that they are running just as hard as the fast guys. Using RPE (rate of perceived exertion) as the measure, the study confirmed that the level of effort is the same for larger runners as it is for the smaller ones. The smaller ones just go faster [88].

The study also confirmed that speed difference between lighter and heavier runners is due to factors other than body fat levels. Even at comparable body fat levels, bigger runners are at a distinct disadvantage.

Weight based divisions exist in seven Olympic sports to make it fair for smaller athletes who are at a disadvantage. In running, the tables are turned and it is the smaller athletes that have the advantage. Adds Hales, "Smaller men flourish in this uniquely, and are guarded and jealous of the weight division competition, believing they are giving away the one sport where their diminutive size is an advantage."

Triathlon does, however, consist of *three* disciplines. Large athletes don't suffer any disadvantage in swimming. Cycling is variable depending upon the course. Small athletes have an advantage on hills, but not so much on flat courses. It is only on the run that large athletes have a clear disadvantage in all distances. Perhaps that is part of the problem. In triathlon, everyone has a weakness. For large athletes, that weakness is always going to be the run.

BMI EVENTS

Weight impacts running performance, but are divisions based on weight alone the best we can do? A new approach is possible using the BMI (Body Mass Index) to determine race divisions. Logistically simple, each competitor records height and weight on the entry form. If done online, software can automatically calculate BMI and place the athlete in a category with his peers.

Says East, "We have held BMI events in the past, and are perfecting this so that we can further level the playing field. Imagine having a 25.5 to 26.4 BMI division. You can even age grade the division. We would have BMI divisions up to about 33 and then go unlimited from there. Categorizing the division in the BMI manner is complicated for most RD's. You will see an emphasis on the BMI method in the future."

DO WEIGHT DIVISIONS HELP?

It is difficult to see a downside to race divisions that encourage participation. Terri, age 47, has raced both as an Athena and in her age-group. "To be honest, I'm completely back of the pack, so I pick which (division) to enter based on which has an earlier swim send off time. Although last season I dropped below the weight to be an Athena. I'm not one of the triathletes that have a strong opinion on the Athena/Clydesdale class in races. I think it can be encouraging to the people who are larger, to not be up against the lean skinny fighting machines."

Scott also likes the weight divisions. "At 235 pounds, I would have been more hesitant racing for the first time against the 150 lb 30-year-olds rather than the variety found in the Clydesdale division. I like the fact that the Clydesdale is sort of split into two "types" of competitors—the muscular, "thick" type and the overweight type. I was the latter, now I'm the former!"

Kevin is 6'1" and weighs 213 pounds. He doesn't race as a Clydesdale, but he thinks the divisions are good for the sport. "I never wanted to be treated differently or be in a special class... but some people are proud to be in the class and want to win something. I think for the people who are motivated by placing in a race this helps level the playing field. Anything that helps get more people moving and active is a good thing."

ELITE CLYDES

Tobjorn Sindballe is known as a big guy. He is among the heaviest professional triathletes, but he is still 24 pounds too light for the Clydesdale division. He weighs 176 lbs. Matty Reed is the world's tallest professional triathlete at 6'5", but at 180 lbs, he's no Clydesdale either.

Heather Wurtele is the real thing. At 6'2" and 152 pounds she towers over her competition. She is the only professional triathlete large enough to qualify for a weight division.

Heather won Ironman Coeur d'Alene in 2008 and is the current Long Course Champion in Canada. After her victory in Canada she answered some questions about weight and triathlon:

INTERVIEW WITH HEATHER WURTELE

This year WTC eliminated weight divisions from all of their North America Races, and they have never had weight divisions at the World Championships in Kona. Do you have any comments about that?

"I have the distinction of being the first, and maybe one of the only female pro triathlete Ironman winners that would qualify as an Athena. (The usual weight requirement is 63.6 kg/140 lb for females. I have less than 10% body fat and at 6'2" I could not get down to 140 lbs without becoming seriously unhealthy.)

It is fantastic that I am a source of inspiration for bigger/taller female athletes. I love hearing "tall chicks rule!" yelled from the sidelines, and I have met a lot of amazing, inspirational women who are proud to be Athena athletes, and who are happy when they have a division where they can compete against other women with their body type.

The Athena/Clyde divisions are controversial because it is unclear who they are really for; thus I can understand why WTC eliminated them. Common perception is that these divisions are for overweight athletes and that they are meant to be inclusive – divisions for athletes that may otherwise feel intimidated to compete because of their size.

There is no doubt that people can be over their ideal body-weight, and still be very fit – having the strength and endurance to complete in Ironman triathlons. Things get tricky with athletes that are well-above average height, and as such fit into the weight categories even when they are super lean. I have felt that if you are super tall, but super fast (able to win your age group overall, for instance) people would accuse you of sandbagging the Athena/Clyde divisions.

With the disappearance of these divisions I think that it is important to remember that what really matters is your own personal improvement over time – not how you compare to others. Having a body that is in shape is much more important than the shape of your body!"

I am sure you watch your nutrition carefully. Do you weigh and measure portions, keep track of the number of grams of given nutrients, anything like that?

"I don't weigh and measure portions, or obsessively track all of my calories, but I am a meticulous reader of labels and nutrition information. I eat primarily plant based foods (lots of veggies!!), and avoid dairy entirely. I try to avoid all processed foods, and I look for very short ingredient lists on those that I do consume (for example granola). If I pick up a product in the store and the ingredients list makes up a paragraph, I don't even bother reading before putting it back on the shelf.

As far as portions go I try never to get overly hungry or overly full. Try being the key word. I still mess up and occasionally bonk during a hard training session or over-eat at the end of a long day – both of these things put your body into fat storage mode, and I want to avoid that."

How often and with what method do evaluate your body composition?

"I usually use the skinny pants method. If I can get into this one pair of jeans, the places where my body tends to store fat are leaner. Kidding. Sort of. I do not weigh myself daily because I have found that it is pretty meaningless and can be self-defeating. I can fluctuate over 10 lbs in the course of a hard training day (not that this is a good thing... I am a very heavy sweater so I need to really stay on top of my hydration to avoid this) and all sorts of things like water retention during menstruation can affect body weight.

If I do a body fat analysis I use the tried and true fat caliper method, and a body fat analyzer scale for confirmation, but I really only get on top of this when it gets close to race season. I am pretty in tune with my body and I can tell when I am getting leaner."

Have you ever made a conscious effort to lose body fat in preparation for a race?

"Yes. I get my husband to refuse to share his treats (chocolate, cookies, etc.) with me, and I don't eat within 2 hrs of bedtime. I also avoid simple carbo-hydrates unless for immediate post-workout recovery. I also try to eat slower and drink more water so I feel satiated quicker."

Being a professional triathlete, do you see that the female pros are in your view, overly concerned about body fat? What about the males?

"I am sure that many athletes suffer from disordered eating – both men and women. Peter Reid has talked about how he would starve himself before Kona to be as lean as possible going into the race.

I think that performing well as a triathlete is important, but I think that my overall health is important too. It is a fine line. You need to be strong for the bike portion of the race, and you don't want to get to the point where you start to sacrifice your power; but the less 'extra' weight you can carry on the run, the easier it is to go fast.

I think that it is important to get to know your own body and not obsess about some super skinny 'ideal' image that others have painted."

Larger athletes are known to have more trouble dissipating heat especially in hot and humid conditions. How do you do in heat? Are there particular strategies you use to manage/minimize overheating?

"In the past I have had real trouble in the heat, and I am constantly working on ways to improve my performance in hot, humid conditions. Training in Victoria, Canada where I wore arm warmers for most rides – even in the height of summer – just didn't cut it for races in Hawaii.

Before races in hot locales I piled on extra clothing while biking and running, and even rode the indoor trainer with the temperature cranked and a humidifier on. This was better than nothing, but still prepared me inadequately for the conditions in Kona.

Now that my husband and I are full time professional triathletes we plan to go somewhere hot and humid for at least a month prior to the world championships to fully acclimatize. You can get used to exerting yourself in all sorts of conditions, it just takes a little time. Turn off the A/C in the daytime, and get used to training in the heat of the day, but make sure you are cool and comfortable at night so that you can sleep well and recover properly.

If you are pale/ have sensitive skin, like myself, it is important to manage UV stress by wearing protective clothing. There are all sorts of excellent sun-proof fabrics on the market now, and it is definitely worth trying a long-sleeve, white Torbjorn Sindballe type outfit... It is also important to get a handle on your sweat rate so that you know how much water and salt you lose while racing. As soon as you start to dehydrate, your performance suffers and you are more likely to overheat."

Pro triathlete Heather Wurtele

What challenges do you face as a larger athlete?

"Other than the heat dissipation issues noted above, I think that my height is an advantage. I have a long stroke in the swim, I am a powerful rider, and my run stride stays strong through the latter stages of the marathon. I do have to work on quick leg turnover during the run, because I had a tendency over-stride, but I've seen runners of all heights are guilty of this one!"

Heather sums it up

"When I first started competing as a pro, I definitely found my competition intimidating and I was very aware that I did not share the body type of a lot of petite, ripped, female pros. I instantly became more successful in my races when I stopped comparing my body to others, and focused on not what I looked like, but what I was able to do!"

15 Weight Loss Supplements

Has anyone seen a wandering Charlatan?
I need a curative potion.

Many triathletes supplement their diets with protein, vitamins and minerals. But what about supplements to help them lose fat? The notion of athletes using substances to enhance weight loss has a long history in weight-class boxing, wrestling and body-building, but triathletes are now coming into the fold. It is hard to say which came first; the athletes willing to buy the magic pills or the manufacturers willing to sell the products. The demand is there. Browse through the pages of triathlete magazines and you will see advertisements for "supplements" to make you leaner.

It is important to look before you leap. Just because a product is labeled as "organic," "natural" or "herbal" does not mean it is safe or effective. In fact, there is reason believe just the opposite is true. A dietary supplement manufacturer does not have to prove a product's safety and effectiveness before it is marketed.

WHAT IS IN IT AND WHAT DOES IT DO?

These are the two most important questions to answer before you take a supplement. Unfortunately, the law is such that supplement manufacturers don't have to accurately answer either question.

WHAT IS IN IT?

Is it safe?

Effective in 2008, large manufacturers were expected to follow certain "good manufacturing practices"(GMP) to ensure that dietary supplements are processed consistently and meet quality standards. In 2012 these expectations will apply to small manufacturers as well. Whether and how these "expectations" will be enforced remains to be seen.

Once a dietary supplement is on the market, the FDA monitors safety. If it finds that a product is unsafe, it can take action against the manufacturer and/or distributor. As time goes on, the safety of dietary supplements is improving but it is still inadequate.

Contaminants

Conventional drugs are free from contaminants [89]. Everything they contain is on the label. Not so with dietary supplements [90]. Supplements may contain undesirable or toxic substances and waste that is not on the label.

Contaminants can include:

- Insects, microbes, and undesirable animal parts. Bovine organs found in supplements may be susceptible to contamination with the agents that cause mad cow disease [91].

- Plants chosen by mistake or the undesirable part of a desired plant. Some plants produce "natural" but dangerous chemicals that can end up in supplements including coumarins (used in anti-coagulants), carcinogens (cancer-causing agents) and tannins (astringents) [92, 93, 94].

- A well known case in 1992 led to the ban of a plant extract (Aristolochic acid) that was accidentally included in a weight loss product in Belgium. Almost

100 patients suffered irreversible renal failure and cancers related to the ingestion of the "tainted" weight-loss supplement [98].

- Heavy metals, pesticides, herbicides and other contaminants from the soil or water that are absorbed by plants [95, 96, 97].

- Added drugs to make you feel good like benzodiazepines, corticosteroids, caffeine and nonsteroidal anti-inflammatory agents.

The processes used in production of some supplements are also poorly regulated [99]. By the time the raw material (plant or animal) enters the manufacturing process, it may have been exposed to a nightmare of contamination like debris, pests, stones, sticks, and other stuff. Many U.S. manufacturers and distributors import raw materials. What are they getting? Current regulations for imported plant and animal products intended for use in dietary supplements does not protect athletes from insufficiently labeled, mislabeled, contaminated or unsafe ingredients [11].

It is nearly impossible to determine what is actually in a dietary supplement. A manufacturer's use of the terms "standardized," "verified" or "certified" does not necessarily guarantee product quality or consistency. About the only thing you can do is purchase from a large "reputable" manufacturer that sends their products to an independent lab for testing and verifying ingredients.

WHAT DOES IT DO?

Claims

How about the second question, "What does it do?" The claimed benefit of a particular supplement need not be proven. Vendors can make health claims about products based on their own review and interpretation of studies without the authorization of the Food and Drug Administration (FDA). The FDA monitors information like label claims once a product is on the market. The Federal Trade Commission (FTC) is responsible for regulating product advertising; it requires that all information be truthful and not misleading.

Weasel-words

We are so used to reading ominous warning labels that we are nearly immune to them. Unfortunately, the tendency to gloss over the bad stuff also makes us less critical of the claimed benefits of a product. Even if the labeling is correct, you should keep in mind the magnitude of product's benefit. Is it worth taking? Consider carefully the language of a claimed benefit. The label on product A that says it "may help reduce appetite" doesn't have much to live up to. There are no promises in the word "may." What does "help reduce appetite" mean? How is it measured? Would you even be able to tell if it was working? "May," "help" and "reduce" are all weasel words.

Compare it to product *B* with a label that says it "will reduce your body fat by 10%". Product *B* has set a high standard of performance; "will" is a guarantee of effectiveness, "body fat" is measurable and "10%" is a significant effect.

Both of the labels (A and B) comply with the FTC requirement that it be truthful and not misleading, but product A is not worth taking.

A manufacturer can claim that a supplement addresses a nutrient deficiency, supports health, or is linked to a particular body function (e.g., immunity), if there is "research" (often the manufacturer's own) to support the claim. The claim must be followed by the words "This statement has not been evaluated by the Food and Drug Administration. This product is not intended to diagnose, treat, cure or prevent any disease." Weasel words.

Even if you find a product that guarantees a significant, measurable benefit (you won't find many), you should still review the research on the product.

Appendix G details steps you should take to evaluate a supplement before you buy it.

WHAT WORKS AND WHAT DOESN'T

Weight loss supplements abound. To analyze them all is a book in itself. Table 14 below lists a few popular supplements, their claims and some scientific information about them. If you intend to take a supplement, investigate it closely on your own first.

Table 14 *Survey of Weight Loss Related Supplements*

*Note: Based on a limited survey of literature at PubMed. Readers are encouraged to evaluate efficacy and safety claims independently and to obtain consent of their physician before taking supplements. Unreferenced material is from www.MayoClinic.com [100].

Substance	Claims	Survey of Science*
Bitter orange	Increases metabolic rate.	Long-term effects unknown. Touted as an "ephedra substitute" but may cause health problems similar to those of ephedra.
Carnitine	Weight loss.	Not taken up by muscle and therefore, not effective [101].
Chitosan	Blocks the absorption of dietary fat.	Can cause constipation, bloating and other gastrointestinal complaints. Relatively safe, but unlikely to cause weight loss.
Cholecystokinin or CCK- a peptide released in the upper intestine during eating which influences satiety.	Appetite Control.	CCK believed to have a role in satiety [102]. Side effects of supplementation include nausea and anxiety [103].
Chromium	Helps build muscle in place of fat.	No supporting evidence of effectiveness.

Conjugated linoleum acid (CAL)	Reduces body fat. Appetite control. Builds muscle.	Can cause diarrhea, indigestion and other gastrointestinal problems. Might decrease body fat and increase muscle, but isn't likely to reduce total body weight.
Country mallow (heartleaf)	Appetite control. Increases metabolic rate.	Contains ephedra, which is dangerous. Likely unsafe and should be avoided.
Ephedra	Appetite Control.	Banned from the marketplace because of safety concerns, but may still be legally sold as a tea. Can cause high blood pressure, heart rate irregularities, sleeplessness, seizures, heart attacks, strokes and even death.
Green Tea, epigallocea-techin-3-gallate (GCG)	Reduces accumulated body fat stores.	Multiple studies showing fat reduction in animals. Limited human studies show effectiveness when combined with caffeine [104].
Guar gum	Blocks the absorption of dietary fat. Appetite control.	Can cause diarrhea, flatulence and other gastrointestinal problems. Relatively safe, but unlikely to cause weight loss.
Hoodia gordonii: contains P57, a supposed appetite-suppressing molecule	Appetite Control.	No published research supporting its long term utility in humans.
Phenethylamine, "Trimspa". Does not list ingredients.	Weight loss.	Associated with multiple troublesome ingredients and side effects include insomnia, migraines, heart palpitations and more [105].

Current information from the Federal Government on the safety of particular dietary supplements is available at *www.fda.gov/Food/DietarySupplements/Alerts/ default.htm* or the "Alerts and Advisories" section of the NCCAM Web site at *nccam.nih.gov/news/alerts*.

NO QUICK FIX

When it comes to weight loss, there is no quick fix. There may be valid reasons to take supplements, but weight loss is not one of them. Triathletes ask so much of their bodies that consuming questionable substances seems foolhardy. Eating less is the safest and most effective way to shed fat. Bernd Heinrich, author and ultra runner summarizes it thus in his book, *Racing the Antelope* [106].

"You can't just increase one function and expect improved performance. Nature does not put in extra parts, nor does she give extra capacities to given parts. You have to improve all the systems at once to affect the whole... improving one part by a simple fix, *even if it actually works*, (sic.) it simply transfers the limiting factor to the next link on a long chain. The one factor that does affect the whole body, all at once and in a coherent, coordinated fashion, is in the mind, where courage comes from. I put more stock in placebos, faith and specific training."

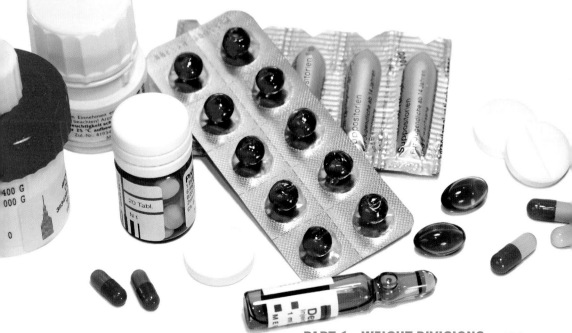

16   What Can Surgery Do?

Marshall Ulrich had his toenails surgically removed
so they wouldn't bother him during ultra marathons.
I had my saddlebags removed so I wouldn't have to carry
them through another Ironman.
If Ulrich can do it, so can I.

– Female Triathlete

COSMETIC SURGERY IS HERE TO STAY

I have never seen an elite triathlete with love handles, a pot belly or saddlebag thighs. It's in the genes, I think. You and I can diet and train till the cows come home and our little flaws and bulges remain. We will never look like them. We will never be as fast as them either, but we try.

Judging from the forum postings on triathlon websites, body shape is high on the list of triathlete concerns. Posters banter back and forth about why they lack muscle definition, whether they look fat in their race photos and how stubborn their bulges of fat are... and that's the men talking!

In the dark days before we became triathletes, our genes and our lives worked together in ways that can make it impossible to attain that lean and shiny look. When you look in the mirror you want to see a triathlete staring back at you. Instead, you see:

- handfuls of extra skin with nowhere to go except over your tri shorts,

- stubborn deposits of fat that hide your six-pack abs, or

- thigh bulges that are simply wrong.

If you are already low on the body fat scale, getting even leaner can be counter-productive and unhealthy. You don't want to develop an eating disorder, wreak havoc on your hormones or negatively impact performance. If you're female, you suffer as your bra size dwindles from small to "don't bother" and it doesn't thrill your husband either. When there is no more fat to lose, surgery is the only way to change your body.

Consider these statistics from the American Society for Aesthetic Plastic Surgery [107]:

- 31% of women and 20% of men say that they would consider some type of cosmetic surgery.

- Most of the surgical cosmetic surgeries are done on 35-50 year olds.

- Liposuction and Abdominoplasty (tummy tuck) are, in the USA, among the most popular procedures for both men and women, exceeding 637,335 in 2007.

- It is not just women that have surgery. In 2007 men had 9 percent of the cosmetic procedures in the United States. Just over 1 million men had cosmetic procedures, up 17 percent from the previous year.

TRIATHLETES STRUGGLE WITH GUILT

Although 78% of the US population says they would not be embarrassed about having cosmetic surgery [108], it remains a subject of controversy, especially for athletes. The ethical issues have been explored in the context of politics, feminism, medicine and religion.

The decision to go under the knife may come after months or even years of wrestling with the ethical issues: is going under the knife selling out? Would a better person be satisfied with the body they have? What will this teach my kids about accepting their own bodies?

The issues are complex. Scott, the triathlete we met in Chapter 11 is still on the fence about it. Having triumphed over alcohol addiction and obesity, he is embarrassed by the large folds of extra skin around his midsection. "I just can't get past the idea of high-stepping into the water at the sound of the bullhorn and having my stomach bounce around that much... let alone coming out of the water with all the spectators and the ubiquitous camera guy!... Nobody knows that I am thinking about surgery. Only one or two of my tri buddies even know I lost weight... Even explaining to one tri friend how I lost 100 lbs. is shameful, let alone that I have extra skin and scars that I want surgically removed."

Dr. Tenley Lawton, a cosmetic surgeon and triathlete, has seen athletes struggle with the idea of surgery to alter their appearance. "I think female athletes especially feel that they should be able to do it themselves. They feel like, "gosh I work this hard, why can't I get rid of this? Athletes feel that cosmetic surgery is too vain and that they have in some way failed because they can't get rid of a particular bulge. They know I am an athlete and they want me to give it to them straight. It helps when I can reassure them and say 'hey, you've done what you can do and that skin is not coming off without surgery.' It takes a load off them."

WHAT CAN SURGERY DO?

Cosmetic surgery is not designed to reduce weight. It is used to enhance, rebuild or repair the body. There are many different procedures that are considered cosmetic, but for the purpose of this book we consider only those related to weight loss like removing extra skin or small pockets of fat.

Even modest weight loss can result in loose skin depending on your age and the condition of your skin. Table 15 details various surgical cosmetic procedures that are related to removal of body-fat and/or excess skin.

Table 15 *Summary of Weight-Related Surgical Cosmetic Procedures**

Surgical Procedures	Best Candidate	Cost**	Length of Procedure
Abdominoplasty (tummy tuck)	Protruding abdomen; excess fat and skin; weak abdominal muscles	$5,350	2-5 hours
Breast Reduction***	Large, heavy, pendulous or disproportionate breasts	$5,417	2-4 hours
Buttock Lift	Sagging skin, excess fat, weakened muscles in thigh/ buttocks area	$4,885	2 hours
Gynecomastia,	Treatment of enlarged male breasts	$3,455	2 hours
(Liposuction) Lipoplasty (suction-assisted) Lipoplasty (ultrasound-assisted)	Normal weight with isolated fatty areas	$2,950	1- 2 hours
Lower Body Lift	Skin laxity without significant fat deposits	$8,043	Up to 8 hours
Thigh Lift	Loose, excess skin	$4,783	2 hours
Upper Arm Lift	Excess skin and fat on underside of arm	$3,864	2 hours

*   Based on American Society for Aesthetic Plastic Surgery for statistical data. 2007 (most recent)

** National average; surgeon fees are based on 2007 Statistics. Fees vary considerably by geographic region. Facility fees, anesthesia and other surgical costs not included.

*** Breast reduction may be covered by insurance, depending on terms of the policy and individual patient factors. Fees may vary.

PROCEDURES FOR MEN

Men have far less cosmetic surgery than women. The most common procedure for men is liposuction which effectively removes "love handles." Liposuction is also helpful for removing excess breast tissue in males, known as gynecomastia.

Lawton recalls one patient, an exceptionally fit man with some extra fat on his chest. "If you looked at the rest of his body you wouldn't believe there was any fat anywhere and he flat out said 'I've done what I can do. I look good everywhere else. I want to be able to take off my shirt without feeling bad.'

The prevalence of tummy tucks (known as abdominoplasty) is growing as bariatric surgery (lap band, gastric bypass) gains popularity. The weight losses following these surgeries are often so dramatic that the skin can't shrink enough so patients turn to cosmetic surgery to remove the excess.

Dan, a 35 year-old age-grouper, had gastric bypass surgery to save his life. He had gained and lost the same 20-40 pounds many times. At 427 lbs "I was starting to battle high blood pressure and was too young to start having major medical problems." Following his 200 pound weight loss, he had 5.5 pounds of extra skin removed.

"I had issues with rashes and poor circulation. Now I look great and feel like a million bucks... I went from a very sedentary lifestyle to one where I race very regularly. I even started a running club at the school where I teach. Without the weight loss surgery, my life would be so different; there is no other way to put it..."

Donald Altman, M.D. has been a cosmetic surgeon for 20 years. He has seen "a tremendous increase in this kind of surgery." The patients have rolls and rolls of extra skin which we can remove. Some that have permanently lost their collagen and skin elasticity have several procedures over the course of a few years. After the surgery some of them are unbelievably attractive, you can't believe that they were ever 350 pounds."

ATHLETES AS PATIENTS

"Athletes make great surgical candidates if they have abided to careful diet and exercise and they have a couple of little bulges that can't be removed through those avenues. Unfortunately, they tend to be less than half of the patients I see. The others are people that can't seem to get diet and exercise under control and want a quick out," says Altman.

"Athletes are highly motivated patients," says Lawton. "They have done all their research and they arrive at the surgeon's office prepared." In the patient's mind, being an athlete is the most important thing about them. She adds, "The very first thing they say when I meet them is... 'I am a runner,' or, 'I am a triathlete and...' Their athleticism defines who they are. It impacts the nature, extent and timing of the procedure they are interested in."

"Having to give up training for awhile it is the one thing that seems to influence the decision about surgery. When I tell a patient that they can't train for a month, they will have to make a big adjustment. I make it easier on them by giving them intermediate goals like: the first week you do nothing. Just hang around the house. After that, you can get back to walking. Sometimes when I say that, their eyes light up 'you mean I can do *something*?' and I tell them 'yes, you can start doing some things with your legs' or whatever depending upon the body part. I give them baby steps and that helps them along."

"I explain," says Altman, "that if a runner sprains an ankle, it takes 6 weeks to heal. The athlete-patient understands that. But to them, cosmetic surgery is different. My job is to convince them that *cosmetic surgery is an injury*. It is a controlled injury, an injury we design, but it still needs to heal."

WHERE DO YOU START?

Anyone considering surgery should investigate thoroughly before making a decision. Read information from several sources about the procedure you are considering. Most surgeons will provide a free or low cost consultation. This will help you decide whether the procedure is right for you, and will inform you about the risks, costs and logistics of the procedure. Meet with several surgeons before you decide.

Look for a surgeon who is board certified with these organizations and one that you are comfortable with:

- The American Society of Plastic Surgeons (ASPS)
- The American Society for Aesthetic Plastic Surgery (ASAPS)

Dr. Altman offers this food for thought. "Plastic surgery is real medicine. It is precision work and 90% of the thought and care that goes into a patient is behind the scenes. It is very hard for a patient to decide where to go and it is hard to get good information. Lots of plastic surgeons have glitzy offices, beautiful websites and gorgeous photos but you have to consider where the surgeon is spending his resources and whether they are delivering a quality product."

"Patients come in for a particular procedure that they heard about in an advertisement. They pick a surgeon who offers the 'new' kind of surgery using 'the latest' surgical tools... Plastic surgery is very technique-oriented and a particular kind of equipment can help a little, but it shouldn't be the deciding factor. Too many companies develop technology then push it on the public... the thing is, I would rather have Tiger Woods playing golf with an old set of clubs than some rookie with the best golf clubs Calloway makes."

"One of the things you do if you are considering extensive surgery that involves lifts or multiple surgical sites, is to ask if there will be an assistant surgeon. The assistant is there to balance the judgment of the surgeon and that additional input is very helpful. It is also important that the assistant have

a level of skill comparable to the primary surgeon. It is an important question to ask," Altman cautions.

ADJUSTING TO A NEW YOU

"Losing 200 pounds in a year doesn't allow your mind to wrap around what is happening to your body." It took Dan 2 years to be able to see the results of his surgery and his hard work in training.

The adjustment is interesting, says Altman "In psychiatry, you might have treatment over many years to solve a problem. But with plastic surgery you can in a day remove something that has been bothering a person for 30 years. It is like 100 therapy sessions come together in a split moment. It's very powerful and in some ways, risky, when you can have demons that have brought you years of pain removed in a couple of seconds. It takes a little while for people accept it."

ACCEPTANCE IS PRICELESS

Surgery, however, will not make you look perfect. No matter what, when you look in the mirror you will find something you would like to change.

Altman adds, "Even if the result isn't exactly what they wanted, people don't have the mental energy to dwell on it forever. A mom with little kids that has a little dimple on her leg may not want it, but you know, you've got to get the kids to school, you've got to do your training. Life goes on."

Surgery or not, at some point we all must come to a point of acceptance. Triathlete Tammy Nickerson says, "I spent several years thinking that it was my fault because I wasn't working hard enough or doing the right mix of strength, cardio and nutrition monitoring... I can see more tone in my legs and upper chest/shoulders area, but nothing changed in the mid section. It was a little discouraging to me, but I've finally realized that I'm doing everything I can. I can stop beating myself up because I'm not working hard enough. I AM working hard enough, but this is the body I have to work with and since I'm not willing to go the surgery route, this is what I have to work with. Sometimes learning to love and accept yourself the way you are is the only thing you can do. It's a hard road, but you're not alone."

SURGERY AND PERFORMANCE

REMOVING EXTRA SKIN

There is an obvious benefit in removing folds of skin that interfere with movement or cause discomfort. If the inside of your thighs rub together when you run, it can cause severe chaffing. Having some fat removed can solve the problem and chances are, you will run better.

When it comes to bike fit, removing loose abdominal skin can change your ability to get into and hold an aerodynamic position. Says aerodynamicist Shayne Kondor in a recent article, "While it could be argued that aero wheels have come a long way in 20 years, shaving some inches off your waist can have equal impact on your bike splits." [109]

Sarah lost 100 pounds with diet and exercise. She had a tummy tuck and is basically happy with the outcome. "I sometimes think about getting my arms done not so much for aesthetics but because the excess skin rubs to the point that it's raw when I swim and run. I am scared of the cost, the pain and I don't want to be laid up for months unable to exercise so I am putting it off."

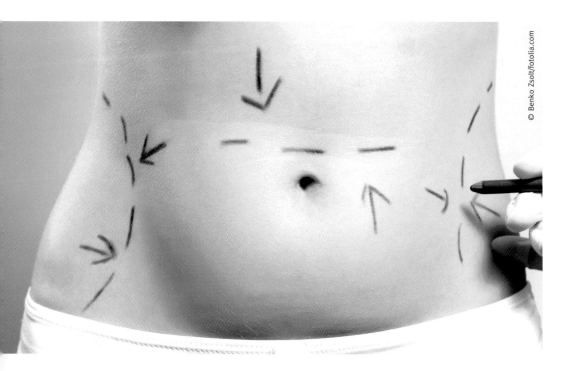

© Benko Zsolt/fotolia.com

REMOVING FAT DEPOSITS

Fat and swimming are troubled bedfellows. Fat is buoyant, which is good. There is evidence, however, that *adding fat* (artificially) to the abdomen, thighs and buttocks of swimmers creates enough drag to trump the buoyancy benefit [110]. If adding fat in to certain places can slow you down, then removing it may make you faster by making you more hydrodynamic.

Personal accounts confirm that significant weight loss alters swimming dynamics. Known anecdotally as 'Lean Man's Syndrome,' parts of the body that used to float nicely will sink like rocks when the fat is gone. Liposuction can alter flotation patterns and drag variables so much that the athlete has learn to swim all over again.

Some research suggests that the location of body fat stores also has an effect on running speed. Based on a study of 184 top-class runners, scientists in Spain concluded that skin fold thickness in the front thigh and medial calf is linked to faster running times [111]. The amount of fat carried subcutaneously at these particular sites on the body was *more important than total amount of body fat*. The reason for this is unclear. Certainly a lower percentage of body fat would be reflected in thinner skinfolds, but this study seems to point to a runner's tendency to carry fat in certain locations as a factor in running speed.

Along these lines, physiologists have added mass artificially to the legs and indeed, added leg loads increase the metabolic rate. Added mass on the upper thigh may increase the metabolic rate due through supporting (via hip abduction muscles) and propagating the swing leg [112].

That said, it does not necessarily follow that removing fat from your legs will make you run faster, but it is fun to consider.

THE PSYCHOLOGICAL IMPACT

The foremost performance benefit from cosmetic surgery is psychological. Solving a problem that has troubled you for years can set you free. Instead of focusing on what is wrong, you can focus on developing as an athlete.

Successful people never underestimate the power of motivation. Feeling satisfied with your body for the first time does not dampen motivation to train, it enlivens it.

When Julie she started doing triathlons, she lost 30 pounds and over a few years, became quite lean. "I was happy with my body but pockets of fat on my upper thighs really got to me. They made by bottom half look like it belonged on a much bigger person. I was amazed that the chunk of fat was still there even when I was 12% body fat. I was at the lower limit of healthy body fat and I did not want to try to get leaner. I was tired of feeling bad about it. I had done all I could, so I had liposuction. It changed my whole outlook and made me love triathlon even more. The sadness is gone and I wish I had done it sooner."

Triathletes that excel do so in large measure because of they believe they can. It is a form of the placebo effect, which is so powerful that scientific studies that test anything from drugs and carbohydrate loading to high-tech running shoes must control for it by testing a group of athletes that *believe* they are using the new product when in truth they are not [113]. If you believe that cosmetic surgery will make you faster, it will.

ONE STEP FURTHER?

In a recent article on Ironman.com, Lee Gruenfeld pokes fun at cosmetic surgery.

"I'm not talking building up your lats or getting liposuction; I'm talking real *sculpting*. Let's say you're a little slow in the water. You can't take steroids to build muscle because those are on the banned list (the steroids, not the muscles), but where does it say that you can't have your local surgeon sew your toes together to turn your feet into a pair of flippers? Mark Spitz's feet look like that but there's no workout that can help you get there, so...?" [114]

One can imagine there will come a time when the line between cosmetic surgery and performance enhancing surgery will blur.

17 Going too Far

A lot of people are afraid of heights.
Not me, I'm afraid of widths.

– Steven Wright

The focus on being lean can sometimes go too far. Sub-clinical levels of eating disorders are common among triathletes. It is unknown whether this is because the sport attracts people prone to these disorders, or because immersion in the sport causes or exacerbates the symptoms.

A 2002 study of 583 triathletes found that *all* of the subjects were dissatisfied with their level of body fat. In the study, participants admitted that they had attempted to reduce body weight by strict dietary rules, calorie restriction, severe limitation of food groups and excessive exercise. Most of the triathletes wanted to be smaller.

The 2002 study, done at the University of North Carolina, also showed that triathletes are prone to misperceptions about their BMI. Males tend to overestimate their actual BMI and women tend to underestimate it. Even with the underestimation, the women wanted to be *much smaller* than they were [115].

Female endurance athletes are known to have body dissatisfaction to the same degree as individuals with anorexia nervosa. Is body dissatisfaction part of what drives them? It is understandable that beginners are especially prone to food preoccupations and body dissatisfaction [116]. Moving from normal life into the world of the super-fit can be a shock to the psyche. Indeed, more experienced triathletes and those that tackle the longer distances are less afflicted with body image woes [116].

At what point does a healthy interest in fitness become a problem? What is the difference between dedication to your sport and a psychological disorder? Pam Reed, ultra runner extraordinaire and the only woman to win the Badwater Ultra marathon outright, twice, has suffered with anorexia. In her book, *The Extra Mile*, she writes,

"One of the things that bothers me about all of the therapies I have had for anorexia is the implication that the 'normal' person is someone who's not excited about, much less totally committed to, anything. I know some people may want to argue with me about this, but to me, what passes for 'normalcy' seems to be the absence of real devotion, not to mention passion. Where would that leave the people who have been the greats in any field? When you have a gift, there is often a dark side. That just seems to be the way things work. One of the biggest challenges of my life has been making sure that the dark side doesn't win." [117]

Triathletes often struggle with the perils of overtraining but they understand that at some point, trying harder is counterproductive. They are so focused on performance that they know immediately when something isn't right. But fanaticism about body image and eating behavior may be harder to recognize. Below is a general discussion of the disorders associated with weight loss in athletes. A detailed list of signs and symptoms of various disorders appears in Appendix H.

EXERCISE ADDICTION

Most triathletes would agree that their passion for the sport and the training is like an addiction, but a positive one. It is important to recognize when training crosses the line from being a positive influence to a negative one. Exercise addiction is not yet a formal disorder recognized by the DSM-1V but it may become one. It often occurs in those with eating disorders but it is more obsessive-compulsive in nature. It is a disorder that at first glance, mirrors the life of a triathlete.

Here are some of the symptoms of exercise addiction that may resemble the habits of a triathlete [122]:

1. Exercising for more than two hours daily, repeatedly.
2. Exercising to the point of pain and beyond.
3. Exercising when sick or injured.
4. Fixation on weight loss or calories burned.
5. Always working out alone, isolated from others.
6. Always following the same rigid exercise pattern.
7. Skipping work, class, or social plans for workouts.
8. Researchers at the University of Cambridge have explored the disorder with an eye toward defining it. Their 2003 paper gives examples and descriptions of symptomatic behavior [118].

They interviewed active women about exercise. This is how a women suffering from the disorder described her exercising:

"I feel it's a great bind. I feel it rules my life and I don't see why I should have to carry this cross when nobody else does."

Subjects were also asked to describe their feelings if they were, hypothetically, prevented from exercising for one week. Here is one of the responses from a woman believed to be suffering from the disorder:

"You wouldn't – you just couldn't do it, well that's what I feel like. You are depriving me of something that is essential to me. You might as well say, "stop eating" or "stop breathing." I should be really depressed, I should be suicidal...

I just wouldn't be able to cope with just sitting in here without exercising. You would probably have to put me in the hospital."

The result of the study was as follows:

1. Attaching a high priority to training is not always problematic and does not necessarily indicate impaired functioning. It is not unusual for competitive athletes to make their training a higher priority than other activities. Athletes are generally able to manage the demands of training successfully with other aspects of life.

2. Mild withdrawal symptoms are common among athletes that are prevented from training. Only severe instances of withdrawal should be regarded as symptomatic.

3. A diagnosis based solely on the amount of exercise is inadequate. A triathlete in the study was clearly not exercise dependent and she reported training seven days a week, often twice daily.

   In contrast, a person with exercise dependence, for instance, has to go up and down a particular staircase for 5 minutes every morning or be in a foul mood all day. Another woman stated that she would be unable to tolerate missing her five to ten minutes of daily weight training and sit-ups.

4. Other troublesome features of the disorder include keeping your training a secret, lying about it or denying it.

5. Those that met the criteria for the disorder dieted to control weight, shape or body composition rather than to improve athletic performance.

These examples point out the differences between exercise addicts and dedicated athletes. It is not the volume of exercise that is a problem, as much as its lack of meaning. Triathletes enjoy training, but it is purposeful. Whether for weight control, performance, or enjoyment, training is not something you are blindly compelled to do everyday. It has meaning to you and that is what makes it worthwhile.

EATING DISORDERS

In the U.S. as many as 10 million women and a million men struggle with anorexia and bulimia. Another 25 million suffer from binge eating disorder [119]. Anorexia, bulimia and binge-eating disorder are all distinct eating disorders.

Anorexia

Anorexics starve themselves. It usually begins around the age of puberty, most often in girls. People suffering from the disorder are very skinny but are convinced that they are overweight. These are the skeleton people you see out running sometimes. Anorexics lose weight with excessive exercise, use of laxatives and refusing to eat.

Bulimia

Bulimia (Bulimia nervosa) is characterized by episodes of out of control binges followed by vomiting, fasting, enemas, excessive use of laxatives and diuretics, or compulsive exercising. A binge is more than just overeating, the person eats a much larger amount of food than most people would in a similar situation and it has nothing to do with hunger but is a response to emotional problems like depression, stress, or problems with self esteem. Bulimia is harder to recognize because the sufferer usually is of normal weight. Women with bulimia tend to be high achievers.

Binge Eating

A person that binges (eats a large volume of food quickly for emotional reasons) has at least 2 binge episodes a week for at least 6 months. They do not purge afterwards like Bulimics. People with binge eating disorder have high personal standards and are preoccupied with weight and food. It is common in older, overweight women but normal weight people can have it too.

A list of symptoms for these disorders appears in Appendix H. Read and answer the online questionnaire at *www.something-fishy.org* if you believe you may suffer from one of them. The following text box illustrates important differences between dieting and eating disorders.

Eating Disorder or Diet?*

The most common element surrounding all eating disorders is the inherent presence of low self esteem. Having an eating disorder is much more than just being on a diet. An eating disorder is an illness that permeates all aspects of each sufferer's life, is caused by a variety of emotional factors and influences, and has profound effects on the people suffering and their loved ones.

Dieting is about losing a little bit of weight in a healthy way.

Eating Disorders are about trying to make your whole life better through food and eating (or lack of).

Dieting is about doing something healthy for yourself.

Eating Disorders are about seeking approval and acceptance from everyone through negative attention.

Dieting is about losing a bit of weight and doing it healthfully.

Eating Disorders are about how life won't be good until a bit (or a lot) of weight is lost, and there's no concern for what kind of damage you do to yourself to get there.

Dieting is about losing some weight in a healthy way so how you feel on the outside will match how good you already feel on the inside.

Eating Disorders are about being convinced that your whole self-esteem is hinged on what you weigh and how you look.

Dieting is about attempting to control your weight a bit better.

Eating Disorders are about attempting to control your life and emotions through food/lack of food—and are a huge neon sign saying "look how out of control I really feel."

Dieting is about losing some weight.

Eating Disorders are about everything going on in life -- stress, coping, pain, anger, acceptance, validation, confusion, fear – cleverly (or not so cleverly) hidden behind phrases like "I'm just on a diet."

* Used by permission from CRC Health. *www.something-fishy.org*

THE FEMALE ATHLETE TRIAD
(EATING DISORDER + MENSTRUAL DYSFUNCTION + OSTEOPOROSIS)

When an eating disorder, amenorrhea and osteoporosis occur together in physically active females, the syndrome is known as the Female Athlete Triad. It starts with training hard and overly restricting calorie intake to maintain a low body weight. This can cause amenorrhea (menstrual dysfunction) [120]. Amenorrhea can be temporary or permanent and can impact on a woman's future ability to have children. Women that suffer this symptom due to under-eating are also prone to stress fractures and osteoporosis.

Achieving and maintaining an unrealistically low body weight is the impetus for development of the Triad. Historically the Triad has been seen in sports that emphasize low body weight for aesthetics, but performance matters too. Sports that require the athlete to defy gravity with jumps (gymnastics); or being thrown, like in pairs figure skating, are easier to do at a low bodyweight. Competitive participants in these sports get started as girls and can find they are fighting a losing battle as they enter puberty. But the disorder is not age-specific. Being lean is also a prerequisite for success in distance running and triathlon which usually attracts participants later in life.

Female triathletes that strive for single digit body fat levels are compromising their health. This tendency was demonstrated in a 2007 study showing that *all* of the female members of a triathlon club team showed symptoms of one or more components of the Female Athlete Triad [121].

If you have one component of the triad (eating disorder, amenorrhea or osteoporosis) you should be screened for the others. The Female Athlete Triad disorders can impair physical performance and cause disease and death [122].

The following information on the Female Athlete Triad was graciously provided by the Female Athlete Triad Coalition at *www.FemaleAthleteTriad.org*.

Risk factors for the Female Athlete Triad:

- Playing sports that require weight checks.
- Social isolation due to sporting activities.
- Exercising more than necessary for a sport.
- Pressure to "win at all costs."

- Punitive consequences for weight gain.
- Controlling parents and/or coaches.
- Being a gymnast, figure skater, ballet dancer, distance runner, swimmer or diver where undue emphasis is placed on having a low body weight and a lean physique.

Common signs and symptoms:
- Irregular or absent menstrual cycles.
- Always feeling tired and fatigued.
- Problems sleeping.
- Stress fractures and frequent or recurrent injuries.
- Often restricting food intake.
- Constantly striving to be thin.
- Eating less than needed in an effort to improve performance or physical appearance.
- Cold hands and feet.
- Please contact the Female Athlete Triad Coalition at *www.FemaleAthleteTriad.org* for more information.

BODY DYSMORPHIC DISORDER

Reuters reported in January 2009 that a growing number of male athletes are developing unhealthy eating behaviors after seeing the competitive advantage a leaner physique can bring. These behaviors are a form of body dysmorphia in male recreational triathletes as well as cyclists and Nordic skiers.

Like exercise addiction, body dysmorphic disorder (BDD) has some symptoms in common with eating disorders but it falls into the category of an obsession or compulsion. It is identified in the DSM-IV as a preoccupation with a "flaw" with your appearance which causes significant distress or impairment in social, occupational or other important areas of your life [123].

It has been called "imagined ugliness" and BDD affects 1-2% of the general population; however, it is a problem that patients are ashamed of so they don't report it to their physicians. The prevalence is probably higher than reported. The disorder generally is diagnosed in those who are extremely critical of their physique or self-image even though there may be no noticeable disfigurement or defect, or a minor defect which is not recognized by most people. One form of the disorder associated with athletes is known as muscle dysmorphia and occurs in men who believe their muscles are underdeveloped.

Donald Altman is a cosmetic surgeon who has seen more of cases of BDD in recent years, although it does not get much publicity. "Body Dysmorphia is a psychiatric disorder and a true sufferer can't even begin to get past their feelings about a body part." When you have body dysmorphic disorder, you obsess over your appearance for hours on a daily basis. You may seek out repeated cosmetic procedures to "fix" the perceived flaw. Says Altman, "If you do surgery, there is always the chance that their attention will shift to another body part. It's like a twitch that won't go away, it just moves. But more than likely they just aren't going to be happy with anything a surgeon does." Part of Altman's job is to identify potential sufferers and to refer them for appropriate help.

A list of additional signs and symptoms of this disorder appears in Appendix H.

TAKE ACTION

If you or someone you care about displays multiple symptoms consistent with any of these disorders, take it seriously and intervene. Suggest they seek an evaluation and if need be, enlist the help of their family members. Contact your family physician for information on referrals. These disorders are dangerous and can be life-threatening.

APPENDIX A: RACE PERFORMANCE WORKSHEET

Best Performances	Weight or body fat %	Weight or body fat %	Worst Performances	Weight or body fat %	Weight or body fat %
Weight when you had your fastest swim performance			Weight when you had your slowest swim performance		
Weight when you had your fastest bike performance			Weight when you had your slowest bike performance		
Weight when you had your fastest run performance			Weight when you had your slowest run performance		
Weight when you placed highest overall in your division			Weight when you placed lowest overall in your division		

APPENDIX B: HOW TO CALCULATE YOUR BETTER THAN EVER WEIGHT FROM BODY COMPOSITION DATA

CALCULATE YOUR BETTER THAN EVER NUMBER

How many pounds of fat do you need to lose to get to your desired body fat %? How much will you weigh at that body fat level? Will your Better Than Ever number be a certain body fat % or a certain weight? It is up to you. In any case, you need to be able to work with your body composition numbers to specify goals.

You can start with a body fat % or with a certain amount of fat you wish to lose. It will work either way.

Here is the formula for determining body fat % from lean and fat weight:

Determine body fat % from lean and fat weight:

A 150 lb athlete with 120 lbs of lean mass and 30 lbs of fat has 20% body fat:

$$\text{Percent body fat} = (\text{fat mass}/\text{total body mass}) \times 100$$
$$\text{Percent body fat} = 30 / 150 \times 100 = 20\%$$

If he loses 16 pounds of fat, his new body fat % will be:

14 lbs of fat/ 134 total pounds x 100 = 10 % body fat

He likes 10%. His Better Than Ever number is 10% body fat or 134 pounds.

APPENDIX C: HOW TO CALCULATE YOUR CALORIE TARGET

FORMULA TO DETERMINE TARGET CALORIE INTAKE

Starting the number of calories you burn per day at rest, (resting metabolic rate or RMR), and add the number of calories you burn per day in training and other activities (energy expenditure or EE) to arrive at your total calorie needs (TCN) to maintain your current weight.

A pound of fat is equivalent to 3500 calories. To lose a pound you must create a deficit of 3500 calories. To lose 10 pounds, 10 x 3500 = 35000 calories and so on.

Total Calorie Needs (TCN) = RMR + EE.
Target Calorie Intake = TCN − 500* or 1000

* Use 500 to lose 1 pound per week or 1000 to lose 2 pounds per week

These and many other sites provide various tools to help you determine your target calorie intake. It is important to know which number you are getting.

RMR: *www.healthstatus.com, www.caloriesperhour.com*
EE: *www.freedieting.com, www.healthstatus.com*
TCN: *www.active.com, www.caloriecount.about.com*
Target calorie intake: *www.freedieting.com, www.healthyweightforum.org*

CALCULATING BY HAND

Calculating your calorie needs by hand requires two steps. First, calculate your resting metabolic rate, RMR, then add your activity calories, EE.

Total Calorie Needs = RMR + EE

1. Calculate your RMR based on body weight

Let's start with RMR. There are various ways to determine your RMR. The most precise, time consuming and expensive way is to have it tested at a lab. You can also calculate it by hand. Different formulas are available, depending on the information you have. If you do not know what your lean body mass is, use the Harris-Benedict [124] formula which is based on total body weight.

Note: 1 inch = 2.54 cm
          1 kg = 2.2 lb

Women: RMR = 655+ (9.6 x wt in kg) + (1.8 x ht in cm) – (4.7 x age in years)
Men: RMR= 66 + (13.7 x wt in kg) + (5 x ht in cm) – (6.8 x age in years)

Example 1:
Using the following athlete:
Male 160 lbs., 160/2.2 = 72.72 kg
5' 10" tall = 70 in x 2.54 = 177.8 cm
Age 40

RMR = 66 + (13.7 x 72.72) + (5 x 177.8) – (6.8 x 40) calories
RMR = 1679.26 calories

2. Calculate RMR based on lean body mass
If you know your lean body mass, use the Katch-McArdle formula which applies to both men and women [126].

RMR = 370 + (21.6 x lean mass in kg.) calories

Example 2:
Same athlete as above, 160 pounds with 140 pounds lean mass:

RMR = 370 + (21.6 x 140 lbs /2.2) calories
RMR = 1744 calories.

Notice how this example 2 shows a higher RMR than example 1, by 65 calories. The formulas provide estimates only so some variation is to be expected.

3. Add your activity calories, EE
The simplest method to incorporate your energy expenditure for movement is to use a multiplier, which is a number based on overall activity levels as outlined on the following page.

Activity multipliers [125]

Activity level	Multiplier
Sedentary-desk job. Little or no exercise.	RMR x 1.2
Light-light exercise/ sports 1-3 days/week	RMR x 1.375
Moderate-mod. exercise/sports 3-5 days/week	RMR x 1.55
Very Active-hard exercise/sport 6-7 days/week	RMR x 1.725
Extreme-hard daily exercise/sports & physical job or 2x day training	RMR x 1.9

Example 3:
Our 160 lb athlete trains 6 hrs/week. He falls somewhere between "Moderate" and "Very Active" in the table. He can either pick a number between the two multipliers, say 1.65, or he can pick one of the categories. Since he wants to lose weight, he is better off underestimating his activity level than overestimating it. He should use the number for the "Moderate" activity level.

Using the Harris-Benedict RMR:
RMR x Moderate activity = Total calorie needs per day
1679 x 1.55 = 2602 calorie per day

Using the Katch-McArdle RMR:
RMR x 1.55 Moderate = Total calorie needs per day
1744 x 1.55 = 2703 calories per day

Using the formulas, our example athlete needs 2600-2700 calories per day to maintain his weight.

ENERGY EXPENDITURE FROM WORKOUTS

If you plan to vary your intake day to day based on training load, you will need to know how many calories are burned in a particular workout. Online calculators can be found at the websites specified above and also *www.howtobefit.com*, or *www.nutristrategy.com*.

Most heart rate monitors and GPS-based computers have calorie expenditure displays as well. You can use them in combination with the chart in Table 16.

Table 16 *Calories expended in triathlon activities each 30 min. based on total body weight.*

30 min. Activity	110 lbs	120 lbs	130 lbs	140 lbs	150 lbs	160 lbs	170 lbs	180 lbs	190 lbs	200 lbs	220 lbs	240 lbs	260 lbs	280 lbs
Bicycling, 13 mph (4.6 min/mile)	220	240	260	280	300	320	340	360	380	400	440	480	520	560
Running (12 min/mile)	203	222	240	259	278	296	315	333	352	370	407	444	481	518
Running (10 min/mile)	253	276	299	322	345	368	391	414	437	460	506	552	598	644
Running, 08 mph (7.5 min/mile)	336	366	396	427	458	488	518	549	579	610	671	732	793	854
Running, 09 mph (6.7 min/mile)	363	396	429	462	495	528	561	594	627	660	726	792	858	924
Running, 10 mph (6 min/mile)	385	420	455	490	525	560	595	630	665	700	770	840	910	980
Swimming (50 yards/min)	248	270	292	315	338	360	382	405	428	450	495	540	585	630
Weight training (60 sec. between sets)	209	228	247	266	285	304	323	342	361	380	418	456	494	532

4. Create a calorie deficit and determine daily calorie target

If you eat the same number of calories that you expend, in our example, 2703, you will stay at the same weight.

If you eat less than the number, you will lose one pound for every 3500 calorie-deficit you create.

To lose 1 pound per week, create a calorie deficit of 500 calories daily. Medical professionals advise creating a deficit of no more than 1000 calories per day, enough to lose 2 pounds/week.

TCN – 1000 = calorie target to lose 2 pounds per week
TCN – 500 = calorie target to lose 1 pound per week

Example 4:
2703 calories/day – 1000 = 1703 calories/day to lose 2 pounds per week
2703 – 500 = 2203 calories/day to lose 1 pound per week.

© arash sabbagh/fotolia.com

APPENDIX D: NUTRITION AND ATHLETIC PERFORMANCE—POSITION OF THE AMERICAN DIETETIC ASSOCIATION, DIETITIANS OF CANADA AND THE AMERICAN COLLEGE OF SPORTS MEDICINE

March 2009 (Volume 109, Issue 3, Pages 509-527)

ABSTRACT

It is the position of the American Dietetic Association, Dietitians of Canada, and the American College of Sports Medicine that physical activity, athletic performance and recovery from exercise are enhanced by optimal nutrition. These organizations recommend appropriate selection of foods and fluids, timing of intake and supplement choices for optimal health and exercise performance. This updated position paper couples a rigorous, systematic, evidence-based analysis of nutrition and performance-specific literature with current scientific data related to energy needs, assessment of body composition, strategies for weight change, nutrient and fluid needs, special nutrient needs during training and competition, the use of supplements and ergogenic aids, nutrition recommendations for vegetarian athletes and the roles and responsibilities of sports dietitians.

Energy and macronutrient needs, especially carbohydrate and protein, must be met during times of high physical activity to maintain body weight, replenish glycogen stores and provide adequate protein to build and repair tissue. Fat intake should be sufficient to provide the essential fatty acids and fat-soluble vitamins, as well as contribute energy for weight maintenance. Although exercise performance can be affected by body weight and composition, these physical measures should not be a criterion for sports performance and daily weigh-ins are discouraged.

Adequate food and fluid should be consumed before, during, and after exercise to help maintain blood glucose concentration during exercise, maximize exercise performance and improve recovery time. Athletes should be well hydrated before exercise and drink enough fluid during and after exercise to balance fluid losses. Sports beverages containing carbohydrates and electrolytes may be consumed before, during, and after exercise to help maintain blood glucose concentration, provide fuel for muscles and decrease risk of dehydration and hyponatremia. Vitamin and mineral supplements are not needed if adequate energy to maintain body weight is consumed from a variety of foods.

However, athletes who restrict energy intake, use severe weight-loss practices, eliminate one or more food groups from their diet, or consume unbalanced diets with low micronutrient density, may require supplements. Because regulations specific to nutritional ergogenic aids are poorly enforced, they should be used with caution, and only after careful product evaluation for safety, efficacy, potency and legality. A qualified sports dietitian and in particular in the United States, a Board Certified Specialist in Sports Dietetics, should provide individualized nutrition direction and advice subsequent to a comprehensive nutrition assessment.

APPENDIX E: GUIDELINES FOR TRAINING-RELATED FUELING

Guidelines for Training-related Fueling [126, 11]

WHEN AND HOW MUCH CARBOHYDRATE TO EAT:

Before Training:
- 4 hrs before, 2 g/lb
- 3 or more hrs. before, 1.5 g/lb (3g/kg)
- 2 hrs before, 1 g/lb
- 1 hr or less before-as tolerated
- Chart below shows calorie recommendations based on body weight

Carb (g/lb)	120 lb (59 kg)	140 lb (63 kg)	160 lb (73 kg)	180 lb (83 kg)	200 lb (91 kg)	220 lb (100 kg)
1 g/lb	480	560	640	720	800	880
1.5 g/lb	720	840	960	1080	1200	1320
2 g/lb	960	1120	1280	1440	1600	1760

During Training:
- At 30 min of low intensity exceeding 2 hr; if high intensity exceeding 1 hr.
- 70 g (280 calories)/hr, every 15-20 min.
- Drink water no matter what.

After Training:
- Eat for recovery if:
  - High intensity at least 60 min.
  - Moderate intensity at least 90 min.
  - Low intensity at least 60 min.
- When to eat:
  - Stage 1:   Within 20 min.
  - Stage 2:   Within 2 hrs.
  - The table below shows recommended calories for Stage 1 and Stage 2 recovery meals.

Stage	Rec. carb intake	120 lb (59 kg)	140 lb (63 kg)	160 lb (73 kg)	180 lb (83 kg)	200 lb (91 kg)	220 lb (100 kg)
1	.5 g/lb	240	280	320	360	400	440
2	.7 g/lb	336	392	448	504	560	616

APPENDIX F: INCREASED CALORIE REQUIREMENTS FOR IRONMAN TRAINING

A typical 24-week training program has a four week cycle; three weeks of increasing volume is followed by one week of reduced volume (3-up, 1-down cycle). Starting with a base of 10 hours/week, training volume increases by about an hour a week. In any 4-week cycle, the training volume increases on average about 2 hours per week. The athlete will eventually build to about 20 hours, but will only have a few weeks at that level. Volumes then decrease into the taper.

If the athlete follows this standard training plan, the volume increases so slowly that by race day, the average training volume is only 5 hours over base level. The athlete goes from a 10 hour average to a 15 hour average. This does not justify a huge or prolonged increase in calorie intake.

Increasing average training volume by 5 hours per week for a 160 pound athlete using 600 calories/hr (an average calorie expenditure for Ironman paced training) increases calorie requirements by 3000 calories per week (5 hr/wk x 600 cal/hr = 3000 cal/wk).

That sounds like a lot. But don't forget to subtract calories consumed during the training sessions. The recommended intake is 280 calories per hour in sessions longer than 2 hours (see Appendix E). Not every session will be that long. There will be some sessions that do not require refueling at all. For discussion's sake, let's say an athlete consumes an average of 200 calories per hour.

During those 5 extra hours of training the athlete will consume 1000 calories. So the 3000 extra calorie deficit is reduced to 2000. (3000 calories expended-1000 calories consumed= 2000 calorie deficit).

2000 extra calories required per week comes out to 286 extra calories a day, enough for a modest recovery meal after training. That isn't much. Ironman training is not a license to eat everything in sight.

APPENDIX G: HOW TO EVALUATE WEIGHT LOSS SUPPLEMENTS

Before you take a supplement, do some research. Here are some things you can do to help you decide whether a particular supplement is safe and effective.

STEP 1: LOOK FOR SCIENTIFIC STUDIES IN PEER-REVIEWED JOURNALS.

On the internet this is as simple as going to *www.PubMed.com* or *www.Medline.com* and entering search words.

PubMed is a public database run by the National Center for Biotechnology Information. It is a service of the U.S. National Library of Medicine and includes over 18 million citations from Medline and other life science journals for biomedical articles back to 1948. It includes links to full text articles and other resources.

Start with the name of the substance. The search will likely turn up anywhere from a handful to hundreds of papers on various aspects of the substance.

As you scroll through the titles of the papers, look for two things:
1. Papers that discuss the training or nutrition benefit of the substance, and
2. Papers that discuss possible harmful effects.

Clicking on the title will bring you an "abstract," or summary of the paper. Scan to the end to see the "Conclusions." If you want to read the entire paper, you will be directed to a site that will charge you a fee for the paper. If you can instead find the email of one of the authors, request a copy directly from them and usually they will happily oblige and will send you a PDF of the article.

For the purpose of your initial investigation, sticking to the abstracts is probably sufficient.

A legitimate supplement manufacturer will base their advertising and claims on the papers that appear at sites like PubMed. If there is no legitimate, peer-reviewed paper to back a claim, the only research you will find will be an article or study done by the manufacturer, published on their own website. This is a red flag and tells you that there is no specific, rigorously tested basis for the claims the manufacturer is making.

If you find papers that support the claims of the manufacturer, proceed to Step 2. If you find papers discussing possible ill effects of the substance and nothing supportive of it, you are done. Don't even consider the product.

STEP 2: EVALUATE THE STRENGTH OF THE RESEARCH

Having found some supporting research is the first step. But research alone is not always helpful. Here are a few things to look for when you evaluate a paper [11]:

✔ Does the study have a clear hypothesis, a clear question that it seeks to answer? Some studies simply give a substance to a few subjects then measure a bunch of variables. The more variables there are, the more they can change. For instance, a substance that seems to improve sprint performance in a 100 meter run will not necessarily improve performance in an Ironman distance triathlon. Did the researcher's test the substance for the benefit you expect it to confer? To improve speed, recovery, fuel utilization, etc.?

✔ Was the study done on humans or on cells? Extrapolating results from cells to humans is a big jump. Look to see what kind of organism the substance was tested on.

✔ If human subjects were used, were they aware of what was being tested? This is known as a "blind" study and it is necessary to eliminate bias. For instance, if subjects volunteered for a study on appetite control, they will have expectations about how a substance will work and those expectations will alter the results of the research. It is best when subjects have no idea what is being evaluated.

✔ Were there control subjects? These are subjects that do not get the tested substance. They get a placebo, which is a dose of sugar or some other innocuous substance. It is important to be able to compare results from subjects that have been given the substance, to those that have not. If the substance causes an effect, there should be a significant difference in results between the subjects that got the placebo (known as the control group) and the subjects that were given the substance.

✔ Were the test subjects like you? A supplement that works on elderly obese subjects with diabetes may not work the same on you. It is not necessary that the research subjects are identical to you, but the subjects should be consistent with the claims of the manufacturer.

✔ Has the same result been reached more than once? If there are several studies, see that they yield similar results.

What if the research is contradictory?
Sometimes research is inconclusive. Several studies will seem to support a particular benefit while others fail to show it. Looking closely at the studies with the above issues in mind may reveal which one seems more reliable, but evaluating the strength of scientific research is not a simple process. When in doubt, don't take the supplement.

If you believe the research is valid, go to Step 3.

If there is decent research on both sides, look closer at the possible harmful effects. If they seem negligible, proceed to Step 3.

STEP 3: LOOK AT THE MANUFACTURER'S WEBSITE

Does the website link to peer reviewed papers that you can find on PubMed? Does it have contact information and assurances about quality control? Do the claims seem reasonable or too good to be true? Use your judgment and evaluate the site as you would a medical site. If it feels like an advertisement for a miracle, don't buy into the hype. If you like what you see, go to step 4.

STEP 4: ASK YOUR DOCTOR

Just to be safe it is a good idea to check with your physician before you start taking anything. Even with your thorough research, you might have missed something. If your doctor say's it is alright and you want to start taking the supplement, find the purest form of the substance. You will have to read labels and shop around.

Ask the manufacturer whether it sends its products to an independent lab for testing and conformance to labeling.

Realize that the reason the manufacturers are trying to sell you a supplement is because they want to make a profit. The manufacturer's job is to entice you to buy the stuff. Whether it works or not is beside the point.

© Daniel Fuhr/fotolia.com

APPENDIX H: SIGNS AND SYMPTOMS OF DISORDERS RELATED TO EXERCISE AND WEIGHT CONTROL

SIGNS AND SYMPTOMS OF ANOREXIA/BULIMIA

Be aware that a sufferer does not need to appear underweight or even "average" to suffer any of these signs and symptoms. Many men and women with Eating Disorders appear not to be underweight. It does not mean they suffer less or are in any less danger.

1. Dramatic weight loss in a relatively short period of time.
2. Wearing big or baggy clothes or dressing in layers to hide body shape and/or weight loss.
3. Obsession with weight and complaining of weight problems (even if "average" weight or thin).
4. Obsession with calories and fat content of foods.
5. Obsession with continuous exercise.
6. Frequent trips to the bathroom immediately following meals (sometimes accompanied with water running in the bathroom for a long period of time to hide the sound of vomiting).
7. Visible food restriction and self-starvation.
8. Visible bingeing and/or purging.
9. Use or hiding use of diet pills, laxatives, ipecac syrup (can cause immediate death!) or enemas.
10. Isolation. Fear of eating around and with others.
11. Unusual food rituals such as shifting the food around on the plate to look eaten; cutting food into tiny pieces; making sure the fork avoids contact with the lips (using teeth to scrap food off the fork or spoon); chewing food and spitting it out, but not swallowing; dropping food into napkin on lap to later throw away.
12. Hiding food in strange places (closets, cabinets, suitcases, under the bed) to avoid eating (Anorexia) or to eat at a later time (Bulimia).
13. Flushing uneaten food down the toilet (can cause sewage problems).
14. Vague or secretive eating patterns.
15. Keeping a "food diary" or lists that consist of food and/or behaviors (i.e., purging, restricting, calories consumed, exercise, etc.)

16. Pre-occupied thoughts of food, weight and cooking.
17. Visiting websites that promote unhealthy ways to lose weight.
18. Reading books about weight loss and eating disorders.
19. Self-defeating statements after food consumption.
20. Hair loss. Pale or "grey" appearance to the skin.
21. Dizziness and headaches.
22. Frequent sore throats and/or swollen glands.
23. Low self-esteem. Feeling worthless. Often putting themselves down and complaining of being "too stupid" or "too fat" and saying they don't matter. Need for acceptance and approval from others.
24. Complaints of often feeling cold.
25. Low blood pressure.
26. Loss of menstrual cycle.
27. Constipation or incontinence.
28. Bruised or calluses knuckles; bloodshot or bleeding in the eyes; light bruising under the eyes and on the cheeks.
29. Perfectionist personality.
30. Loss of sexual desire or promiscuous relations.
31. Mood swings. Depression. Fatigue.
32. Insomnia. Poor sleeping habits

SYMPTOMS OF BINGE EATING DISORDER

1. Fear of not being able to control eating, and while eating, not being able to stop.
2. Isolation. Fear of eating around and with others.
3. Chronic dieting on a variety of popular diet plans.
4. Holding the belief that life will be better if they can lose weight.
5. Hiding food in strange places (closets, cabinets, suitcases, under the bed) to eat at a later time.
6. Vague or secretive eating patterns.
7. Self-defeating statements after food consumption.
8. Blames failure in social and professional community on weight.
9. Holding the belief that food is their only friend.
10. Frequently out of breath after relatively light activities.
11. Excessive sweating and shortness of breath.
12. High blood pressure and/or cholesterol.
13. Leg and joint pain.

14. Weight gain.
15. Decreased mobility due to weight gain.
16. Loss of sexual desire or promiscuous relations.
17. Mood swings. Depression. Fatigue.
18. Insomnia. Poor sleeping habits.

* Used by permission from CRC Health. *www.something-fishy.org*

SYMPTOMS OF BODY DYSMORPHIC DISORDER**

- Obsessive thoughts about perceived appearance defect.
- Obsessive and compulsive behaviors related to perceived appearance defect (see section below).
- Major depressive disorder symptoms.
- Delusional thoughts and beliefs related to perceived appearance defect.
- Social and family withdrawal, social phobia, loneliness and self-imposed social isolation.
- Suicidal ideation.
- Anxiety; possible panic attacks.
- Chronic low self-esteem.
- Feeling self-conscious in social environments; thinking that others notice and mock their perceived defect.
- Strong feelings of shame.
- Avoidant personality: avoiding leaving the home, or only leaving the home at certain times, for example, at night.
- Dependant personality: dependence on others, such as a partner, friend or parents.
- Inability to work or an inability to focus at work due to preoccupation with appearance.
- Decreased academic performance (problems maintaining grades, problems with school/college attendance).
- Problems initiating and maintaining relationships (both intimate relationships and friendships).
- Alcohol and/or drug abuse (often an attempt to self-medicate).
- Repetitive behavior such as constantly applying make up and often applying it quite heavily.
- Seeing slightly varying image of self upon each instance of observation in mirror/reflective surface.

Common compulsive behaviors associated with BDD include:

- Compulsive mirror checking, glancing in reflective doors, windows and other reflective surfaces.
- Alternatively, an inability to look at one's own reflection or photographs of oneself; often the removal of mirrors from the home.
- Attempting to camouflage imagined defect: for example, using cosmetic camouflage, wearing baggy clothing, maintaining specific body posture or wearing hats.
- Excessive grooming behaviors: skin-picking, combing hair, plucking eyebrows, shaving, etc.
- Compulsive skin-touching, especially to measure or feel the perceived defect.
- Becoming hostile toward people for no known reason, especially those of the opposite sex.
- Reassurance-seeking from loved ones.
- Excessive dieting and exercise.
- Self harm.
- Comparing appearance/body-parts with that of others, or obsessive viewing of favorite celebrities or models that the person suffering from BDD wishes to resemble.
- Use of distraction techniques: an attempt to divert attention away from the person's perceived defect, e.g. wearing extravagant clothing or excessive jewelry.
- Compulsive information seeking: reading books, newspaper articles and websites which relate to the person's perceived defect, e.g. hair loss or dieting and exercise.
- Obsession with plastic surgery or dermatology procedures, with little satisfactory results for the patient.
- In extreme cases, patients have attempted to perform plastic surgery on themselves, including liposuction and various implants, with disastrous results. Patients have even tried to remove undesired features with a knife or other such tool when the center of the concern is on a point, such as a mole or other such feature in the skin.
- Excessive enema use.

** Body Dysmorphic Disorder Sources [127, 128]

REFERENCES

[1] Lebenstedt M, Platte P, Pirke KM. (1999). Reduced resting metabolic rate in athletes with menstrual disorders. *Med Sci Sports Exerc*. 31(9): 1250-1256.

[2] Kirschenbaum DS. (2000). *The 9 Truths about Weight Loss: The No-Tricks, No-Nonsense Plan for Lifelong Weight Control*. Henry Holt, p. 22.

[3] Yang MU, Van Itallie TB. (1976). Composition of weight lost during short-term weight reduction. Metabolic responses of obese subjects to starvation and low-calorie ketogenic and nonketogenic diets. *J Clin Invest*. 58(3): 722-30.

[4] Wadstrom C, Backman L, Forsberg AM, Nilsson E, Hultman E, Reiszenstein P, Ekman M. Body composition and muscle constituents during weight loss: studies in obese patients following gastroplasty. (2000). *Obesity Surgery* 10(3): 203-213.

[5] Nicklas BJ, Wang X, You T, Lyles MF et al. (2009). Effect of exercise intensity on abdominal fat lass during calorie restriction in overweight and obese post menopausal women: a randomized, controlled trial. *Am J Clin Nutr*. 89(4): 104-52. Epub 2009 Feb 11.

[6] Ballor DL, Poehlman ET. (1994). Exercise-training enhances fat-free mass preservation during diet-induced weight loss: a meta-analytical finding. *Int J Obes Relat Metab Disord*. 18(1): 35-40.

[7] Stiegler P, Cunliffe A. The role of diet and exercise for the maintenance of fat-free mass and resting metabolic rate during weight loss. (2006). *Sports Med*. 36(3): 239-62.

[8] Deibert P, Konig D, Vitolins MZ, et al. (2007). Effect of a weight loss intervention on anthropometric measure and metabolic risk factors in pre-versus post menopausal women. *Nutr J*. 6:31.

[9] Gordon MM, Bodd MJ, Ester L, et al. (2008). Effect of dietary protein on the composition of weight loss in post-menopausal women. *J Nutr Health Aging*. 12(8): 505-9.

[10] Van Loan MD, Keim NL, Barbieri TF & Mayclin PL. (1994). The effects of endurance exercise with and without a reduction of energy intake on fat-free mass and the composition of fat-free mass in obese women. *European Journal of Clinical Nutrition* 48(6): 408-15

[11] Jeukendrup A, & Gleeson, M. (2004). *Sport Nutrition*. Human Kinetics.

[12] Williams, J. (2009). *Shape up with the Slow Fat Triathlete*. Da Cappo Press

[13] Forster JL, Jeffery RW. (1986) Gender differences related to weight history, eating patterns, efficacy expectations, self-esteem, and weight loss among participants in a weight reduction program. *Addict Behav*. 11(2): 141-7.

[14] Lebenstedt M, Platte P, Pirke KM. (1999). Reduced resting metabolic rate in athletes with menstrual disorders. *Med Sci Sports Exerc.* 31(9): 1250-1256.

[15] Kirk EP, Jacobsen DJ, Gibson C, Hill JO, Donnelly JED. (2003). Time course for changes in aerobic capacity and body composition in overweight men and women in response to long-term exercise: the Midwest Exercise Trial (MET). *Int J Obes Relate Metab Disord.* 27(8): 912-9.

[16] Arrese AL, Ostariz ES. (2006). Skinfold thicknesses associated with running performance in highly trained runners. *J Sport Sci.* 24:69-76.

[17] Bale P, Rowell S, Colley E. (1985). Anthropometric and training characteristics of female marathon runners as determinants of distance running performance. *J Sports Sci.* 3: 115-126.

[18] Bunc V, Heller J, Horcic J, Novotny J. (1996). Physiological profile of best Czech male and female young triathletes. *J Sports Med Phys Fitness.* 36(4): 265-70.

[19] Sleivert GG, Rowlands DS. (1996). Physical and physiological factors associated with success in the triathlon. *Sports Med.* 22(1): 8-18.

[20] Knechtle B, Knechtle P, Rosemann T. (2009). Skin-fold thickness and training volume in ultra-triathletes. *Int J Sports Med.* 30: 343-347.

[21] Landers GJ, Blanksby BA, Ackland TR, Smith D. (2000). Morphology and performance of world championship triathletes. *Ann Hum Biol.* 27(4): 387-400.

[22] Chatard JC, Padilla S, Cazorla G, Lacour R. (1985). Influence of body height, weight, hydrostatic lift and training on the energy cost of the front crawl. *NZ Sports Med.* 13: 82-84.

[23] Pendergast DR, Di Prampero PE, Craig AB Jr, Wilson DR, Rennie DW. (1977). Quantitative analysis of the front crawl in men and women. *J Appl Physiol.* 43(3): 475-9.

[24] Costill DL, Kovaleski J, Porter D, Kirwan J, Fielding R, King D. (1985). Energy expenditure during front crawl swimming: predicting success in middle-distance events. *Int J Sports Med.* 6(5): 266-70.

[25] MacLaren D, Reilly T, Lees A. (1992). *Biomechanics and Medicine in Swimming: swimming science VI.* Taylor & Francis.

[26] Holmér I. Oxygen uptake during swimming in man. (1972). *J Appl Physiol.* 33(4): 502-9.

[27] Bassett DR, Kyle CR, Passfield L, Broker JP, Burke ER. (1999). Comparing cycling world hour records, 1967-1996: modeling with empirical data. *Med Sci Sports Exerc.* 31(11): 1665-1676.

[28] Padilla S, Mujika I, Cuesta G, Polo JM, Chatard JC. (1996). Validity of a velodrome test for competitive road cyclists. *Eur J Appl Physiol Occup Physiol.* 73(5): 446-51.

[29] Padilla S, Mujika I, Cuesta G, Goiriena JJ. (1999). Level ground and uphill cycling ability in professional road cycling. *Med Sci Sports Exerc.* 31(6): 878-85.

[30] Wilson RS, James RS. (2004). Constraints on muscular performance: trade-offs between power output and fatigue resistance. *Proc Biol Sci.* 7: 271 *Suppl.* 4: S222-5.

[31] Selkirk GA, McLellan TM. (2001). Influence of aerobic fitness and body fatness on tolerance to uncompensable heat stress. *J Appl Physiol.* 91: 2055-2063.

[32] Reynolds WW, Karlotski WJ. (1977). The Allometric Relationship of Skeleton Weight to Body Weight in Teleost Fishes: A Preliminary Comparison with Birds and Mammals. *Copeia,* 160-163.

[33] Varady KA, Santosa S, Jones PJ. (2007).Validation of hand-held bioelectrical impedance analysis with magnetic resonance imaging for the assessment of body composition in overweight women. *American Journal of Human Biology: the official journal of the Human Biology Council.* 19(3): 429-33.

[34] Swan PD, McConnell KE. (1999). Anthropometry and bioelectrical impedance inconsistently predicts fatness in women with regional adiposity. *Med Sci Sports Exerc.* 31(7): 1068-75.

[35] Varady KA, Santosa S, Jones PJ. (2007). Validation of hand-held bioelectrical impedance analysis with magnetic resonance imaging for the assessment of body composition in overweight women. *Am J Hum Biol.* 19(3): 429-33.

[36] Collins MA, Millard-Stafford ML, Sparling PB, et al. (1999). Evaluation of the BOD POD for assessing body fat in collegiate football players. *Med Sci Sports Exerc.* 31(9): 1350-1356.

[37] Heyward, VH. Evaluation of body composition.Current Issues. (1996). *Sports Medicine.* 22(3): 146-56.

[38] Jackson AS, Ellis KJ, McFarlin BK, Sailors MH, Bray MS. (2009). Cross validation of generalized body composition equations with divers young men and women: the Training Intervention and Genetics of Exercise Response (TIGER) Study. *Br J Nutr.* 101(6): 871-8. Epub 2008 Aug 15.

[39] Hellemans I. (1999). Maximizing Olympic Distance Triathlon Performance: A Sports Dietitian's Perspective. Proceedings from the Gatorade International Triathlon Science II Conference, Noosa, AU, 11/7-11/8.

[40] Jeukendrup, A & Gleeson M. (2004). *Sport Nutrition.* Human Kinetics, p. 281.

[41] Le Carvennec M, Fagour C, Adenis-Lemarre E, Perlemoine C, Gin H, Regalleau V. (2007). Body composition of obese subjects by air displacement plethys-mography: The Influence of Hydration. *Obesity* (Silver Spring). 15(1): 78-84.

[42] Fields DA, Higgins PB, Hunter GR. (2004). Assessment of body composition by air-displacement plethysomography: influence of body temperature and moisture. *Dynamic Medicine.* 3(1): 3.

[43] Virnig AG, McLeod CR. (1996). Attitudes toward eating and exercise: A comparison of runners and triathletes. *Journal of Sport Behavior.* 19: 82-90.

[44] Ryan M. (2007). *Sports Nutrition for Endurance Athletes.* VeloPress.

[45] United States Olympic Committee website. (retrieved 3/2009).

[46] Shephard RJ, & Astrand PO. (1992). *Endurance in Sport.* Blackwell Scientific Publications, p.254.

[47] Lopez P, Ledoux M, Garrell DR. (2000). Increased thermogenic response to food and fat oxidation in female athletes: relationship with VO_2 max. *Am J Physiol Endocrinol Metab.* 279: E601-7.

[48] Abbot JM, Thomson CA, Ranger-Moore J, Teixeira PJ, et al. (2008). Psychosocial and behavioral profile and predictors of self-reported energy under-reporting in obese middle-aged women. *J Am Diet Assoc.* 108(1): 114-9.

[49] Sorrento RM, Higgins ET. (1990). *Handbook of Motivation and Cognition, Vol 2: Foundations of Social Behaviour.* Guilford Press, p 135-136.

[50] Polivy J, Herman CP. Dieting and Binging: A causal analysis. (1985). *American Psychologist.* 40: 193-201.

[51] Burton P, Smith HJ, Lightowler HJ. (2007). The influence of restrained and external eating patterns on overeating. *Appetite.* 49(1): 191-7.

[52] Cooling J, Blundell J. (1998). Are high-fat and low-fat consumers distinct phenotypes? Differences in the subjective and behavioral response to energy and nutrient challenges. *Eur J Clin Nutr.* 52(3): 193-201.

[53] Rolls B. (2009). The relationship between dietary energy density and energy intake. *J.Physiol Behav.* 97(5): 609-15. Epub 2009 Mar 20.

[54] Latner JD, Rosewall JK, Chisholm AM. (2009). Food volume effects on intake and appetite in women with binge-eating disorder and weight-matched controls. *Int J Eat Disord.* 42(1): 68-75.

[55] De Castro JM. (1993). The effects of the spontaneous ingestion of particular foods or beverages on the meal patterns and overall nutrient intake of humans. *Physiol. Behav.* 53: 1133-1144.

[56] Bellisle F, Drewnowski A. (2007). Intense sweeteners, energy intake and the control of body weight. *Euro J Clin Nutr.* 61(6): 691-700. Epub 2007 Feb. 7.

[57] Haapala I, Barengo NC, Biggs S, Surakka L, Manninen P. (2009).Weight loss by mobile phone: a 1-year effectiveness study. *Public Health Nutr.* 1-10.

[58] Van Weir MF, Ariens GA, Dekkers JC, Hendriksen IJ, Smid T, van Mechelen W. (2009). Phone and e-mail counseling are effective for weight management in an overweight working population: a randomized controlled trial. BMC *Public Health.* 9:6.

[59] Butryn ML, Phelan S, Hill JO, Wing RR. (2007). Consistent self-monitoring of weight: a key component to successful weight loss maintenance. *Obesity.* 15(12): 3091-6.

[60] Tanake M, Itoh K, Abe S, et al. (2004). Irregular patterns in the daily weight chart at night predict body weight regain. *Exper Bio and Med.* 229: 940-945.

[61] National Weight Control Registry, www.nwcr.ws (retrieved August 2009).

[62] Miller-Kovach K, Hermann M, Winick M. (1999). The psychological ramifications of weight management. *J Womens Health Gend Based Med.* 8(4): 477-82.

[63] Raben A, Agerhlom-Larsen L, Flint A, Holst JJ, Astrup A. (2003). Meals with similar energy densities but rich in protein, fat, carbohydrate, or alcohol have different effects on energy expenditure and substrate metabolism but not on appetite and energy intake. *American Journal of Clinical Nutrition.* 77: 91-100.

[64] Why alcohol calories are more important than you think. *www.thefactsaboutfitness.com* (retrieved July 2009).

[65] Kovacs, Betty MD, RD. Alcohol and Nutrition. *www.Medicinenet.com.* (retrieved 7/6/2009.)

[66] Heikkonen E, Ylikahri R, Roine R. Valimaki M, et al. (1996). The combined effect of alcohol and physical exercise on serum testosterone, leutenizing hormone, and cortisol in males. Alcoholism, Clinical and Experimental Research. 20: 711-716.

[67] Kvist H, Hallgen P, Jonsson L, et al. (1993). Distribution of adipose tissue and muscle mass in alcoholic men. *Metabolism.* 42: 569-573.

[68] Guerrieri R, Nederkoorn C, Jansen A. (2008). The interaction between impulsivity and a varied food environment: its influence on food intake and overweight. *Int J Obes.* (Lond). 32(4): 708-14. Epub 2007 Dec 4.

[69] Ackroff K, Bonacchi K, Magee M, Yiin YM, Graves J, Sclafani A. (2007). Obesity by choice revisited: Effects of food availability, flavor variety and nutrient composition on energy intake *Physiol Behav.* 92(3): 468-78. Epub 2007 Apr 24.

[70] Raynor HA, Jeffrey RW, Phelan S, Hill JO, Wing RR. (2005). Amount of food group variety consumed in the diet and long-term weight loss maintenance. *Obesity Res.* 13(5): 883-90.

[71] Soenen S, Westerterp-Plantenga MS. (2008). Proteins and satiety: implications for weight management. *Curr Opin Clin Nutr Metab Care.* 11(6): 747-51.

[72] Westerterp-Plantenga MS, Nieuwenhuizen A, Tome D, Soenen S, Westerterp KR. (2009). Dietary protein, weight loss, and weight maintenance. *Annu Rev Nutr.* Apr 27 (Epub ahead of print).

[73] Ballor DL, Poehlman ET. Exercise-training enhances fat-free mass preservation during diet-induced weight loss: a meta-analytical finding. (1994). *Int J Obes Relate Metab Disord.* 18(1): 35-40.

[74] Ballor DL, Katch VL, Becque MD, Marks CR. (1988). Resistance weight training during caloric restriction enhances lean body weight maintenance. *American Journal of Clinical Nutrition.* 47(1): 19-25.

[75] Cook Gray. (2005). *Athletic Body in Balance.* Human Kinetics, p. 9.

[76] Stroud M. (1998). The nutritional demands of very prolonged exercise in man. *Proceedings of the Nutrition Society.* 57: 55-61.

[77] McElroy M. (2002). *Resistance to Exercise: A Social Analysis of Inactivity.* Human Kinetics, p. 26.

[78] White P, Young K, Gillett J. (1995). Bodywork as a moral imperative: Some critical notes on health and fitness. *Society and Leisure.* 18: 159-182.

[79] Blaine BE, Rodman J, Newman JM. (2007).Weight loss treatment and psychological well-being: a review and meta-analysis. *J Health Psychol.* 12: 66-82.

[80] Wing RR, Phelan S. (2005). Long-term weight loss maintenance. *Am J Clin Nutr.* (82) (suppl):222S-5s.

[81] Yue G, Cole KJ. (1992). Strength increases from the motor program-comparison of training with maximal voluntary and imagined muscle contractions. *J Neurophysiol.* 67(5): 1114-23.

[82] Teixeira PJ, Going SB, Houtkooper LB, Cussler EC, Blew RM, Sardinha LB , et al. (2006). Exercise motivation, eating, and body image variables as predictors of weight control. *Med Sci Sports Exerc.* 38(1): 179-188.

[83] National Weight Control Registry, *www.nwcr.ws* (retrieved July 2009).

[84] Gilbert JA, Drapeau V, Astrup A, Tremblay A. (2009). Relationship between diet-induced changes in body fat and appetite sensations in women. *Appetite.* 52(3): 809-12. Epub 2009 Apr 21.

[85] McLean JA, Barr SI. (2003).Cognitive dietary restraint is associated with eating behaviors, lifestyle practices, personality characteristics and menstrual irregularity in college women. *Appetite.* 40: 185-192.

[86] *www.thesaurus.reference.com/browse/tenacity#visualthesaurus* (retrieved July 29, 2009).

[87] Vanderburgh PM, Crowder TA. (2006). Body mass penalties in the physical fitness tests of the Army, Air Force, and Navy. *Mil Med.* 171(8): 753-756.

[88] Crecelius AR, Vanderburgh PM, Laubach LL. (2008). Contributions of body fat and effort in the 5K run: age and body weight handicap. *J Strength Cond Reser.* 22(5): 1475-1480.

[89] Center for Drug Evaluation and Research. 21 C.F.R. Parts 210 and 211. *www.fda.gov/cder/dmpq/cgmpregs.htm* (retrieved July 2009).

[90] Cole MR, Fetrow CW. (2003). Adulteration of Dietary Supplements. *Am J Health System Pharm.* 60: 1576-1580.

[91] U.S. Department of Agriculture. Detention without physical examination of bulk shipments of high-risk tissue from BSE-countries – bovine spongiform encephalopathy. Import alert #17-04. *www.fola.gov/ora/fiars/ora _import _ ia1704.html* (accessed 2003 Apr 23).

[92] Huggett DB, Khan IA, Allgood JC, et al. (2001). Organochlorine pesticides and metals in select botanical dietary supplements. *Bull Environ Contam Toxicol.* 66: 150-5.

[93] Heaney RP. (2000). Lead in calcium supplements: cause for alarm or celebration? *JAMA.* 284: 1432-3.

[94] Malawska M, Wilkomirski B. (2001). Accumulation rate of polychlorinated biphenyls (PCBs) in dandelion (Taraxacum officinale) in the conditions of soil contamination with oil derivatives. *Rocz Panstw Zakl Hig.* 52: 295-311.

[95] D'Arcy PF. (1991). Adverse reactions and interactions with herbal medicines. Part 1. Adverse reactions. *Adverse Drug React Toxicol Rev.* 10: 189-208.

[96] Ernst E. (1988). Harmless herbs? A review of the recent literature. *Am J Med.* 104: 170-8.

[97] Bartels CL, Miller SJ. (1998). Herbal and related remedies. *Nutr Clin Pract.* 12: 5-19.

[98] Healy M. (2009, May 25). Here's what's in those weight-loss supplements. Los Angeles Times. Retrieved July 2009, from *www.articles.latimes.com/2009/may/25/health/he-supplements-list25*.

[99] Evans WC. (2002). *Trease & Evans' pharmacognosy.* 15th ed. Philadelphia: W. B. Saunders, pp. 55-94.

[100] Over-the-counter-weight-loss-pills: Do they work? May Clinic Staff. *www.MayoClinic.com.* Retrieved 7/17/09.

[101] University of Maryland Medical Centre. (2002). *www.umm.edu/altmed/articles/carnitine-l-000291.htm.* Retrieved 5/20/2008.

[102] Neary MT, Batterham RL. (2009). Gut hormones: Implications for the treatment of obesity. *Pharmacol Ther.* Epub ahead of print.

[103] Greenough A, Cole G, Lewis J, Lockton A, Blundell J. (1998).Untangling the effects of hunger, anxiety, and nausea on energy intake during intravenous cholecystokinin octapeptide (CCK-8) infusion. *Physiol. Behav.* 65: 2.

[104] Maki KC, Reeves MS, Farmer M, Yasunaga K, Matsuo N, Katsuragi Y, Komikado M, Tokimitsu I, Wilder D, Jones F, Blumberg JB, Cartwright Y. (2009). Green tea catechin consumption enhances exercise-induced abdominal fat loss in overweight and obese adults. *J Nutr.* 139(2): 264-70. Epub 2008 Dec 11.

[105] Wong C. (2007) Does Trimspa Work? What you need to know about Trimspa diet pills, updated: September 19, 2007 *www.About.com.* Retrieved June 2009.

[106] Heinrich, Bernd. (2001). *Racing the Antelope: What Animals Can Teach Us About Running and Life.* HarperCollins, p.73.

[107] Health Statistics Plastic Surgery procedures (per capita) (most recent) by country. *www.Nationmaster.com.* Retrieved 6/2009.

[108] America's general approval of cosmetic surgery. American Society for Aesthetic Plastic Surgery 2008. *www.surgery.org.* Retrieved August 2009.

[109] Kondor S. (2009). Aerodynamics – What is it worth to you? *www.TheSportfactory.com.* Retrieved June 2009.

[110] Lowensteyn I, Signorile JF, Giltz K. (1994). The Effect of Varying Body Composition on Swimming Performance. *Journal of Strength and Conditioning Research.* 8(3): 149-154.

[111] Arrese AL, Ostariz ES. (2006). Skinfold thicknesses associated with running performance in highly trained runners. *J Sport Sci.* 24: 69-76.

[112] Browning RC, Modica JR, Kram R, Goswami A. (2007). The effects of adding mass to the legs on the energetics and biomechanics of walking. *Med Sci. Sports Exerc.* 29: 515-525.

[113] McClung M, Collins D. (2007). Because I know it will: placebo effects of an ergogenic aid on athletic performance. J Sport Exerc Psychol. 29(3): 382-94.

[114] Gruenfeld, L. (2008). from *Beyond Beyond: The Next Unnatural Step.* 9/28/08 Ironman.com. Retrieved May 2009.

[115] DiGioacchino DR, Wethington H, Sargent R. (2002). Body size dissatisfaction among male and female triathletes. *Eating and Weight Disorders.* 7(4): 316-323.

[116] Debate RD, Turner M, Flowers C, Wethington H. (2002). Eating attitudes, body image, and nutrient intake in female triathletes. *Women Sport Physl* Act J.

[117] Reed P. (2006). *The Extra Mile.* Rodale Books, p. 26.

[118] Bamber DJ, Cockerill IM, Rodgers S, Carroll D. (2003). Diagnostic criteria for exercise dependence in women. *Br J Sports Med.* 37: 393-400.

[119] National Eating Disorders Association. (2009). *www.nationaleatingdisorders.org.* Retrieved July 2009.

[120] Loucks, AB. (2003). Energy availability, not body fatness, regulates reproductive function in women. *Exerc Sport Sci Rev.* 31: 144-8.

[121] Hoch AZ, Stravakos JE, Schimke JE. (2007). Prevalence of female athlete triad characteristics in a club triathlon team. *Arch Phys Med Rehabil.* 88(5): 681-2.

[122] Otis CL, Drinkwater B, Johnson M, Loucks A, Wilmore J.(1997). American College of Sports Medicine position stand. The Female Athlete Triad. Med Sci Sports Exerc. 1997 May; 29(5): i-ix. Comment in: *Med Sci Sports Exerc.* 29(12): 1669-71.

[123] *Diagnostic and Statistical Manual of Mental Disorders, Fourth Edition.* (1994). American Psychiatric Association.

[124] Harris J, Benedict F. (1919). *A biometric study of basal metabolism in man.* Washington D.C. Carnegie Institute of Washington.

[125] Katch, Frank, Katch, Victor, McArdle, William. (1996). *Exercise Physiology: Energy, Nutrition, and Human Performance, 4th edition.* Williams & Wilkins.

[126] Ryan M. (2007). *Sport Nutrition for Endurance Athletes.* Velopress.

[127] Philips, KA. (2005). *The Broken Mirror,* Oxford University Press.

[128] Mayo Clinic. *http://www.mayoclinic.com/health/body-dysmorphic-disorder/DS00559.* Retrieved June 2009.

ABOUT THE CONTRIBUTORS...

Alan Couzens, MS (Sports Science) is an Exercise Physiologist & Coach currently working at Endurance Corner's Human Performance Lab in Boulder, Colorado. *www.alancouzens.blogspot.com/www.endurancecorner.com*

Donald A., Altman, M.D.
Diplomate American Board of Plastic Surgery
Diplomate American Board of Otolaryngology – Head and Neck Surgery
Daipsc@aol.com

Tenley Lawton, M.D.
Diplomate American Board of Plastic Surgery
TenleyLawton@hotmail.com

Drs. Altman and Lawton can be reached at:
Irvine Plastic Surgery Center
16300 Sand Canyon Ave. Suite 1011 Penthouse
Irvine, CA 92618

Jim Herkimer, MS, MPT, ATC
Executive Director of SCAR
Sports Conditioning and Rehabilitation
871 S. Tustin Ave.
Orange, CA 92866
(714) 633-7227
www.scarpt.com
Jimherkimer@scarpt.com

PHOTO & ILLUSTRATION CREDITS

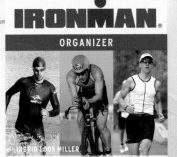
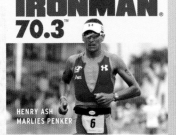

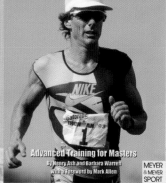